Hettner-Lectures, 1

Explorations in critical human geography

HETTNER-LECTURES

Series Editors: Hans Gebhardt and Peter Meusburger

Managing Editor: Michael Hoyler

Hettner-Lectures, 1

Department of Geography, University of Heidelberg

1998

EXPLORATIONS IN CRITICAL HUMAN GEOGRAPHY

Hettner-Lecture 1997

with

Derek Gregory
Department of Geography
University of British Columbia
Vancouver, Canada

Department of Geography, University of Heidelberg

1998

Copyright © Department of Geography, University of Heidelberg 1998. All rights reserved.

First published 1998

Department of Geography
University of Heidelberg
Im Neuenheimer Feld 348
D-69120 Heidelberg
Germany

http://www.geog.uni-heidelberg.de

Cover illustration: Seminar: Lutz Nücker; Map 'Cairo': International map of the world, sheet NH-36; Derek Gregory: Lutz Nücker; Villa Bosch: Klaus Tschira Foundation; Alfred Hettner: Department of Geography, Heidelberg; Departmental building: Michael Hoyler; Seminar: Lutz Nücker; Painting Heidelberg c. 1840: Kurpfälzisches Museum, Heidelberg; Seminar: Lutz Nücker.

All black-and-white photographs in this volume by Lutz Nücker

Printed in Germany by Druckagentur Jürgen-J. Sause, Heidelberg

ISBN 3-88570-501-X

Contents

Introduction: Hettner-Lecture 1997 in Heidelberg PETER MEUSBURGER and HANS GEBHARDT	3
Power, knowledge and geography DEREK GREGORY	9
The geographical discourse of modernity DEREK GREGORY	45
Discussing imaginative geographies: Derek Gregory on representation, modernity and space MICHAEL HOYLER	71
Klaus Tschira Foundation	107
Photographic representations: Hettner-Lecture 1997	113
List of participants	121

INTRODUCTION

Introduction: Hettner-Lecture 1997 in Heidelberg

PETER MEUSBURGER and HANS GEBHARDT

The Department of Geography, University of Heidelberg, held its first "Hettner-Lecture" from June 23-27, 1997. This new annual lecture series, named after Alfred Hettner, Professor of Geography in Heidelberg from 1899 to 1928 and one of the most reputable German geographers to the day, is devoted to new theoretical developments in the borderlands between geography, economics, the social sciences, and the humanities.

During his stay, the invited guest-speaker presents two public lectures, one of which is transmitted via teleteaching on the internet. In addition, several seminars give graduate students and young researchers the opportunity to meet and converse with an internationally acclaimed scholar. Such an experience at an early stage in the acadamic career opens up new perspectives for research and encourages critical reflections on current theoretical debates and geographical practice.

The first Hettner-Lecture was given by Professor Derek Gregory, University of British Columbia, Vancouver. Since the publication of his *Ideology, science and human geography* (1978), Derek Gregory's project of a critical human geography has continued to emphasise the need for the socialisation of our discipline and the spatialisation of social theory. Reinterpreting and questioning prominent theoretical debates in his *Geographical imaginations* (1994), he reflects on the interplay between political economy, social theory, cultural studies, and geography. His most recent work explores the historical geography of Egypt and colonial representations of landscape, space and people. During the Hettner-Lecture 1997 Derek Gregory presented his challenging ideas in two public lectures entitled "The geographical discourse of modernity" and "Power, knowledge and geography".[1]

Four seminars with graduate students and young researchers from Heidelberg and various other German, Austrian and Swiss universities took up issues raised in the lectures. The rooms and gardens of the *Villa Bosch*, built above Heidelberg Castle in the 1920s, provided a wonderful ambience and creative setting for discussion and reflection. In order to encourage active participation, all seminars included group work and started with visual introductory material. Spontaneous thoughts were recorded and (re)structured with the help of Metaplan moderation techniques. The four sessions with Derek Gregory were headed 'Geographical representations', 'Theorising space', 'Modernisation, modernity and the city' and 'Mapping space'.

---

[1] "Power, knowledge and geography", *Hörsaal der Physik*, Monday, 23rd June 1997, 15.15; "The geographical discourse of modernity", *Alte Aula der Universität*, Tuesday, 24th June 1997, 11.15; afterwards reception, *Bel Etage, Rector's Office*.

Both public lectures and extracts from the seminars appear here in our new publication series "Hettner-Lectures" together with a short photographic recollection of the event in June 1997.[2] Our deep appreciation goes to Derek Gregory, who took the risk of being the first Hettner-Lecturer, kindly responded to ever increasing demands from our side and made the Hettner-Lecture 1997 a wonderful experience for all participants.

The generosity of the *Klaus Tschira Foundation* enabled us to inaugurate this lecture series at a time when the quality of teaching and research at our universities is threatened by decreasing financial resources. We should like to express our gratitude to Dr. hon. Klaus Tschira for his active interest in research frontiers of our discipline. Moreover, we gratefully acknowledge the foundation's offer to be their first guests in the newly renovated *Villa Bosch*. We also thank the Rector of Heidelberg University, Prof. Dr. Peter Ulmer, for providing the *Alte Aula* and *Bel Etage*, and the Vice-Rector, Prof. Dr. Norbert Greiner, for his welcome address at the opening ceremony.

Heidelberg students and young faculty members committed themselves to making the first Hettner-Lecture a success. We owe special thanks to Heike Jöns for professionally co-ordinating the organisational work and to Tim Freytag and Michael Hoyler for their creative way of moderating the seminars. Grischa Pfister and Alexander Zipf, backed by the Department of Physics, mastered the technical challenge of transmitting the Hettner-Lecture via MBone live on the internet. Holger Köppe, Lutz Nücker and Hans-Georg Siebig were responsible for documenting the event on photographs and video,[3] Katharine Reynolds took on the transcription of the seminar discussions, Stephan Scherer provided valuable technical assistance with the preparation of the manuscripts for print. Last but not least thanks to all involved students for their help and active participation during the Hettner-Lecture 1997.

---

[2] "Power, knowledge and geography" will also be printed in volume 86 (1998) of the *Geographische Zeitschrift*, continuing a tradition of publishing theoretically informed research, instigated over a hundred years ago by Alfred Hettner, the journal's founding editor.

[3] A video containing both public lectures is available from the Department of Geography.

POWER, KNOWLEDGE AND GEOGRAPHY

Power, knowledge and geography*

DEREK GREGORY

> 'Writing picture post-cards to his Indian friends, he felt that all of them would miss the joys he experienced now, the joys of form, and that this constituted a serious barrier. They would see the sumptuousness of Venice, not its shape, and though Venice was not Europe, it was part of the Mediterranean harmony. The Mediterranean is the human norm. When men leave that exquisite lake, whether through the Bosphorus or the Pillars of Hercules, they approach the monstrous and extraordinary; and the southern exit leads to the strangest experience of all. Turning his back on it yet again, he took the train northward....'
>
> E.M. Forster, *A Passage to India*

Geography, 'European science' and Eurocentrism

'Power, knowledge and geography' is a phrase that I first noticed in the writings of Edward Said, where it was mapped in luminous detail in his critique of Orientalism. The phrase also conjures up the work of the French philosopher Michel Foucault, who once conceded to the editors of the journal *Hérodote* that geography necessarily lay at the heart of his concerns. These parallels raise many questions, of course, not least about the debt that Said once owed to Foucault and about the possibility of its redemption. My own purpose in drawing them is to confront, as directly as I can, the conjunction between Eurocentrism and European high theory, and to use this triangle between power, knowledge and geography to deconstruct another: the triangle between 'Geography, European science and Eurocentrism'.

In David Stoddart's spirited reflections on geography and its history, his central thesis – one whose passion animated all of the essays in that extraordinary book – is that modern geography is a constitutively *European* science whose formation belongs to the closing decades of the eighteenth century. The decisive moment was, so he

---

* This essay has been revised in the course of successive presentations at the Annual Meeting of the Canadian Association of Geographers, at the University of California at Berkeley, at the University of Bristol, and at the University of St Andrews in Scotland. On those occasions I learned much from the constructively critical comments of Paul Glennie, Elspeth Graham, Cindi Katz, Donald Moore, Chris Philo, Allan Pred, Neil Smith, Nigel Thrift, Michael Watts and Charles Withers. I owe a special debt to Dan Clayton who worked through an early (and far from satisfactory) manuscript and made a series of wonderfully perceptive and challenging suggestions: I only wish I could do them justice in the confines of a single essay. Something very close to the present version was delivered as the first Hettner-Lecture at the Ruprecht-Karls-Universität in Heidelberg in June 1997. I am indebted to the generosity of the Klaus Tschira Stiftung for making my visit possible, and to Peter Meusburger both for his warm hospitality in a rain-soaked Heidelberg and for a series of wonderfully engaging discussions with him, his colleagues and graduate students throughout my stay.

suggests, Cook's entry into the Pacific in 1769. The work of the scientists, collectors and illustrators who accompanied him displayed three features that Stoddart takes to be of strategic importance for the formation of geography as a modern empirical science: realism in description, systematic classification in collection, and the comparative method in explanation. Their efforts were not confined to adventures in natural history, however, and Stoddart's pivotal claim is that it was 'the extension of scientific methods of observation, classification and comparison to peoples and societies that made our own subject possible.' The formation of modern geography as an objective science was propelled by Reason, advancing first into the wide world of Nature and then, turning back on itself, and confronting its mirror image in the consideration of Culture.[1] I will want to complicate these characterizations in due course, but Stoddart's is not an exceptional view. Although David Livingstone's chronology is different, his reconstructions of 'the' geographical tradition – in the singular – also privilege Europe and marginalise (for example) Arab and Chinese traditions of geography.[2] In neither case do I dissent from the claim that modern geography *is*, in its transnational hegemonic forms, a 'European' science – on the contrary – but I do quarrel with intellectual histories that ignore the ways in which these constitutive exclusions and erasures have been secured and which fail to consider the consequences of their closures.[3] Like Gillian Rose, I believe that the construction of such a 'tradition' involves the production of a specular spatiality – a territory 'into which some are gathered and from which others are exiled'[4] – but, unlike her, I want to interpret territoriality in a stubbornly literal sense to insist that this European science is also a profoundly *Eurocentric* science.

This argument is another version of the distinction Foucault drew in *The order of things* between 'the history of the Other' – the history of that which a cultural formation excludes and closes off – and what he called 'the history of the Same': 'the history of the order imposed on things and collected into identities.'[5] For this reason I don't propose to focus on the raw instrumentality of modern geography and its direct complicity in the projects of European colonialism through the production of topographic maps, the compilation of resource inventories, and the logistics of

---

[1] David Stoddart, *On geography and its history* (Oxford: Blackwell, 1986).

[2] David Livingstone, *The geographical tradition: episodes in the history of a contested enterprise* (Oxford and Cambridge, MA: Blackwell, 1992).

[3] 'European science' it may be, but it is important to acknowledge the part played by subaltern groups and indigenous knowledges in its historical formation, including the involvement of non-Europeans as guides, interpreters and informants. Such a project will also require us to read surviving European-language texts 'against the grain' to recover the silences and resistances buried within them.

[4] Gillian Rose, 'Tradition and paternity: same difference?' *Transactions, Institute of British Geographers* 20 (1995) pp. 414-416.

[5] Michel Foucault, *The order of things* (London: Tavistock, 1970) p. xxiv.

colonial government and military power.⁶ Instead I want to disclose a series of *conceptual modalities* and to show that Eurocentrism carries within itself a system of what I call 'geo-graphs' that order its representations. Again, Foucault helps make this clearer. In the closing sections of *The order of things* one commentator finds not what he calls 'the usual moral argument against Eurocentrism' – vitally important though that is – but rather an analysis of

> 'the predicates which make it possible. Setting aside the question of its morality, it was no mean conceptual feat to organize the entire surface of the globe according to a particular system of knowledge. Foucault himself described his analysis in *The order of things* in terms of this incorporation of the other into the same, of the history of the order imposed on things by European culture. *The order of things* could be seen as an analysis not of Eurocentrism as such, but of its philosophical and conceptual archaeology. Before we can undo Eurocentrism, before we can undermine its continuing power, we have to understand how it was done.'⁷

This can I think be pressed still further. To understand 'how it was done' involves, as Foucault's own archaeologies and genealogies showed, a spatial analytics that does not treat space as an empty surface marked by the inscriptions of power and knowledge but which discloses the implication of spatiality in the *production* of power and knowledge. To be sure, the conditions of possibility that underwrite these productions are not purely discursive. But in confining our histories to the empirical work carried out by explorers and adventurers, field scientists and natural historians, cartographers and surveyors, district officers and travellers, in all their dense materiality; in animating our histories with the busy, practical and thoroughly cosmopolitan world of late eighteenth- and nineteenth-century Europe which is the main concern of contextual disciplinary histories like Stoddart's, and the avowedly critical histories of geographical knowledge that have been proposed in his wake: in making all of these necessary reconstructions, and yet sliding over the conceptual orders that were implicated in these very practices, it becomes deceptively easy to fall into the assumption that all of these things belong to the past. Hand-wringing turns surreptitiously into hand-washing. The belief that 'the past is another country, they do things differently there' is one of the vital provocations for historical inquiry, but if it becomes a license for erasing continuities it cannot serve as an effective goad for a critical history of the present. In elucidating the *conceptual orders* of Eurocentrism, in disclosing some of the ways in which power, knowledge and geography were brought

---

⁶ See, for example, Anne Godlewska and Neil Smith (eds.), *Geography and empire* (Oxford UK and Cambridge MA: Blackwell, 1994); Morag Bell, Robin Butlin and Michael Heffernan (eds.), *Geography and imperialism 1820-1940* (Manchester: Manchester University Press, 1995).

⁷ Robert Young, 'Foucault on race and colonialism', *New Formations* 25 (1995) pp. 57-65; quotation from pp. 61-2. See also his *White mythologies: writing History and the West* (London and New York: Routledge, 1990).

together under its sign, it becomes much more difficult to assume that we have left such predicaments behind, and much more likely that we will be forced to recognise that Eurocentrism and its geo-graphs continue to invest our geographies with their troubling meanings.[8]

The subject of Europe: Adventures in historical geography

I need to fix, in a rough and ready way, the historical co-ordinates of my argument. Like Stoddart, I focus on the late eighteenth and nineteenth centuries, but I do so for different reasons. Let me begin with Agnes Heller's audacious claim that a 'specifically European identity was not formed before the eighteenth century' and that it was, in large measure, a paradoxical product of modernity during the long nineteenth century: as she puts it, 'Modernity, the creation of Europe, itself created Europe.' Heller's purpose in advancing this claim was to counter what she saw as the 'mythology' of Europe as a descendant from the classical civilizations of Greece and Rome, in the course of which 'Europe created a culture of its own, and grew different branches of the tree of its culture, which turned out to be the supreme culture of recorded history.'[9]

I sympathise with Heller's objection, but if we are to grasp the power of Eurocentrism we must acknowledge the imaginative reach – the cultural reality – of this mythology. The term is perfectly appropriate. The idea of Europe – what John Hale calls, in a wonderfully disconcerting phrase, 'the discovery of Europe' – did not assume a coherent and programmatic form until the fifteenth and sixteenth centuries. But it did so in part through the activation of a classical mythology. Medieval scholars had been familiar with the classical figure of 'Europe', but Hale doubts whether most ordinary inhabitants had ever heard of the word. The common appeal was to 'Christendom', which also carried within it multiple recognitions of the legacy and authority of Rome.[10] The early modern expansion of Europe into the New World continued to be framed by these symbolic allegiances. Patricia Seed has shown that when the different European powers claimed colonial rights over the New World between 1492 and 1650, they did so through radically different ceremonies of possession that involved a truly disparate array of cultural signs.

---

[8] I hope it will be allowed that the contrast between an 'empirical history' and a history of concepts is a polemical one; a critical history of geographical knowledge has to incorporate both moments in order to recover the sutures and tensions between 'thought-and-action'.

[9] Agnes Heller, 'Europe: an epilogue?' in Brian Nelson, David Roberts and Walter Veit (eds.) *The idea of Europe: problems of national and transnational identity* (New York: Berg, 1992) pp. 12-25.

[10] John Hale, 'The discovery of Europe', in his *The civilization of Europe in the Renaissance* (London: HarperCollins Publishers, 1993) pp. 3-50; see also Gerard Delanty, 'Europe in the age of modernity', in his *Inventing Europe: idea, identity, reality* (London: Macmillan, 1995) pp. 65-83.

'Englishmen held that they acquired rights to the New World by physical objects, Frenchmen by gestures, Spaniards by speech, Portuguese by numbers, Dutch by description.' And yet all of them invoked Roman expansion and Christian supremacy as their root-metaphors, even if these were understood in different ways: they all appealed to what Seed calls 'the myth of a common Europe'.[11] During the Renaissance Hale argues that this myth had taken on a novel and even palpable reality. The creative arts from pottery to painting allegorized the Greek myth of Europa's abduction by Jupiter, and the congress between these two figures – 'the toughest of the planets' and 'the most dominant of continental queens', as Hale calls them – did much to help establish the ideological supremacy of Europe.[12]

But Hale also shows that the most persuasive and powerful images of all were derived from a second thematic which emerged out of an alliance between an ascendant cartography and a detailed chorography that at last enabled Europeans to form a credible wor(l)d-picture of the continent in which they lived.[13] It is the subsequent development of this second thematic – the formation of geography as a modern, empirical science – that engages Stoddart's attention, but this science, like the cultural formation in which it was embedded, was marked by power, self-confidence and assertion, and also by wonder, self-doubt, and anxiety. More than this: flickering on the periphery of Stoddart's vision, and on occasion disrupting the direction of his argument, is an imaginative, figurative language that continued to invest his supposedly strictly 'empirical science' with meaning and legitimation.

These processes constituted more than the discipline of geography, however, and I want to reverse Stoddart's gaze in order to consider the non-disciplinary geographies – the geo-graphs – that were carried within what became, in the course of the nineteenth century, a larger Eurocentric *project*. This is why I think Heller was right to focus on the late eighteenth and nineteenth centuries, because it was then that the seminal conjunction between the figurative and the empirical was consolidated in a geographical imaginary that constituted the 'subject of Europe' in a new and exceedingly powerful configuration. For Heller the central generating mechanism was a post-Enlightenment capitalist modernity which imprinted a distinctively Eurocentric 'vision' on the world.[14] Her emphasis on visuality seems to me exactly

---

[11] Patricia Seed, *Ceremonies of possession in Europe's conquest of the New World, 1492-1650* (Cambridge: Cambridge University Press, 1995) pp. 179-193.

[12] Hale, 'Discovery of Europe' *op. cit.*, pp. 14-15.

[13] Ibid., p. 27. See also John Gillies, *Shakespeare and the geography of difference* (Cambridge UK: Cambridge University Press, 1994); Lesley Cormack, *Charting an empire* (Chicago: University of Chicago Press, 1997).

[14] Heller, *op. cit.*; for a different – and I think reductive – construction of Eurocentrism as a 'canonical culture of capitalism', see Samir Amin, *Eurocentrism* (New York: Monthly Review Press, 1989).

right, even if it remains a highly general model: other scholars have elected to identify the importance of determinate 'visual economies' and 'scopic regimes' to the formation of nineteenth-century modernity.[15] My preference is to show that this Eurocentric 'vision', which was focal to a sense of European identity, was installed through a constellation of four geo-graphs that entered into the formation of an intrinsically *colonial modernity*. They were: (1) absolutizing time and space; (2) exhibiting the world; (3) normalizing the subject; (4) abstracting culture and nature.

I identify each of them in the most active of forms – 'absolutizing', 'exhibiting', 'normalizing', 'abstracting' – in order to emphasize that these are discursive *practices*: that Eurocentrism was not just an idea and that the accounts drawn up under its sign had acutely material consequences. The history of concepts that I have in mind fastens on connections between systems of power and spaces of knowledge, so that concepts are not purely intellectual devices. Foucault borrowed the idea of a 'history of concepts' from Georges Canguilhem, but he gave it a specific twist. For Canguilhem concepts corresponded to disciplines, whereas Foucault's archaeology traded on concepts that were transdisciplinary in scope. To be sure, in his early writings these systems of concepts were supposed to form a coherent and systematic structure, an *episteme*, whereas my own sense of intellectual fabric is much more ragged than that. But as I consider each of these four threads in turn, it will become clear that they were braided into one another in intricate and tensile ways, that they reached far beyond the confines of any formal discipline and that they entered into the constitution of a distinctively modern discursive formation in something very much like Foucault's sense of that term.

Two cautions before I proceed. First, it would be quite wrong to conclude that these four characterizations summarise all European thought. Eurocentrism, for all its imperial ambitions, is mercifully not the totality of European culture. Even then, my account is necessarily selective. I focus on Britain and British colonialism because that is the legacy that dominates my own present and the one that I know the best. There were, of course, other colonialisms, and Eurocentrism was shaded in complex ways by national rivalries and petty chauvinisms. Secondly, it would also be a mistake to assume that these four geo-graphs emerged fully-formed in the nineteenth century; on the contrary. But I do think that it was during the long nineteenth century that they became woven together within an intrinsically colonial modernity.

---

[15] See, for example, Deborah Poole, *Vision, race and modernity: a visual economy of the Andean image world* (Princeton: Princeton University Press, 1997); Martin Jay, 'Scopic regimes of modernity', in his *Force-fields: between intellectual history and cultural critique* (London and New York: Routledge, 1988) pp. 115-133.

Absolutizing time and space

When I speak of 'absolutizing' time and space I am not thinking of the technical concept of absolute space as 'a distinct, physical and eminently real or empirical entity in itself.' I have taken this definition from an elegant essay by James Blaut in which he shows how such a concept of absolute space has occupied a central place in the history of geographical thought. Blaut's point was essentially philosophical. He claimed that the concept had failed to sustain an adequate understanding of process.[16] So it had; but the failure involved more than philosophy and more, I think, than the concept of absolute space.

Power, knowledge and geography were bound together under the sign of Eurocentrism through a discursive system that at once subsumed and discriminated between several different concepts of time and space. In my view, the project of colonial modernity depended crucially on the production and generalisation of *abstract space*, which involved securing not so much the rationalisation *of* space as an identity between Reason *and* Space.[17] The sovereignty of abstract space was inscribed within the play of power and desire, and so I speak of 'absolutizing' time and space in order to invoke a metaphorical association with the political absolutism of early modern Europe: in order to describe a spiralling circle of domination but also, and equally important, to convey its underlabouring ideology of completion and legitimation. The work done by this ideological formation was extremely important. Abstract space was a powerful construction not only because, as Henri Lefebvre once proposed, it was 'the space of the commodity', and not only by virtue of its constellation of what he called the 'visual-phallic-geometric'.[18] Both of these were immensely significant, of course, but the colonising production of abstract space also required the prosecution of concepts through which European metrics and meanings

---

[16] James Blaut, 'Space and process', *Professional Geographer* 13 (1961) pp. 1-7.

[17] Derek Gregory, *Geographical imaginations* (Oxford UK and Cambridge MA: Blackwell, 1994) p. 131.

[18] Henri Lefebvre, *The production of space* (Oxford UK and Cambridge MA: Blackwell, 1991). I do not mean to deny the power of these two characterizations. Eurocentrism is rather more (and rather less) than the commodity culture of European capitalism, but when H.M. Stanley's account of his travels *In Darkest Africa* celebrated the commodity form as what Thomas Richards calls 'a fluid medium that could traverse the continent with no insuperable impediment' it certainly conjured up the colonial space of the commodity. And when Anne McClintock re-presents the same symbolic landscape she forcefully captures the play of desire across the same space. 'In the flickering magic lantern of imperial desire, teas, biscuits, tobaccos, Bovril, tins of cocoa and, above all, soaps, beach themselves on far-flung shores, tramp through jungles, quell uprisings, restore order and write the inevitable legend of commercial progress across the colonial landscape.' See Thomas Richards, 'Selling Darkest Africa', in his *The commodity culture of Victorian England: advertising and spectacle, 1851-1914* (Stanford: Stanford University Press, 1990) pp. 119-167; quotation from p. 128; Anne McClintock, 'Soft-soaping empire: commodity racism and imperial advertising', in her *Imperial leather: race, gender and sexuality in the colonial contest* (London and New York: Routledge, 1995) pp. 207-231; quotation from p. 219.

of 'History' and 'Geography', each with their own imperial capital, were taken to be natural and inviolable, as marking the single centre around which it was meet and proper to organise other histories and other geographies. This is what I mean by 'absolutizing time and space'.

I assume that this (or something very much like it) is what Simon Ryan had in mind when he described 'the space of empire' as 'universal, Euclidean and Cartesian, a measurable mathematical web':

> 'The imperial endeavour encourages the construction of space as a universal, measurable and divisible entity, for this is a self-legitimising view of the world.... Constructing a monolithic space allows imperialism to hierarchise the use of space to its own advantage. In imperial ideology the Aborigines do not have a different space to that of the [European] explorers; rather they under-utilise the space imperialism understands as absolute.'[19]

Ryan was describing the colonial relation between Europe and Australia, and I will retain his focus on the continental level of the absolutization of space. I want to pay particular attention to the production of Europe as a sovereign subject at the centre of an imaginative grid that positioned all the other continents in subordinate spaces. Although this has been called the 'myth of continents', and with justification, I must repeat that myths are not insubstantial fantasies.[20] On the contrary, they have resolutely material consequences, and the constructions that concern me here were carried forward, in different ways and in different forms, in myriad colonial policies and practices. This has to be emphasized or what follows will seem implausibly pure. The imaginative geographies that were embedded in European colonial projects were much muddier than I can convey in this simple argumentation-sketch.

The conventional metanarrative has Eurocentrism absolutizing time and space by folding two distinctions together: one between 'the West' and 'the non-West', and the other between 'History' and what Eric Wolf called 'the people without History' (Figure 1).[21] In a philosophical register these oppositions can be traced through the work of a number of eighteenth- and nineteenth-century writers, but perhaps the most systematic architect of these absolutisms was Hegel. In his *Lectures on the philosophy of history,* which he first delivered in the winter of 1822-23, Hegel conceded that global geometries were relative – 'every country is both east and west in relation to others' – but he argued that it was History that transformed those co-ordinates into the absolute configuration of world Geography. 'World History travels from

---

[19] Simon Ryan, *The cartographic eye: how explorers saw Australia* (Cambridge: Cambridge University Press, 1996) p. 4.

[20] Martin Lewis and Kären Wigen, *The myth of continents: a critique of metageography* (Berkeley: University of California Press, 1997).

[21] Eric Wolf, *Europe and the people without history* (Berkeley: University of California Press, 1982); Wolf's title was, of course, ironic.

east to west,' he declared, 'for Europe is the absolute end of history, just as Asia is the beginning.'[22]

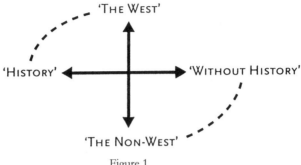

Figure 1

Put most succinctly, 'beyond Europe' was also 'before Europe'.[23] As the language of my last paragraph indicates, the usual way in which this assumption and its variants have been described privileges History. Indeed, in an influential essay Johannes Fabian argued that 'geopolitics' was based on 'chronopolitics'. In his view, the importance of the Enlightenment was that it inaugurated a break from the Judaeo-Christian narrative of time as salvation and incorporation, and enacted a distinction between 'culture' and 'civilization' that eventually issued in the secularization of time as progress. This secular model underwrote the late nineteenth-century triumph of what Anne McClintock describes as 'the image of global history consumed, at a glance, in a single spectacle from a point of privileged invisibility' – in other words, from Europe – and this produced in its turn what she calls 'anachronistic space'. She sees this as a device for inscribing disavowal. The agency of figures whose marginality was marked by class, gender and colonial subjection was projected onto and placed within a space of alterity which was constructed, so McClintock says, as 'prehistoric, atavistic and irrational, *inherently out of place in the historical time of modernity.*'[24]

---

[22] G.W.F. Hegel, *Lectures on the philosophy of history* (Cambridge: Cambridge University Press, 1975 edn.), pp. 190, 197. It is, inevitably, a composite Hegel who speaks to us in the published version of these lectures, which has been compiled from his own (incomplete) manuscripts and the detailed notes of several different students. There are also important differences between Hegel's first presentations in 1822-23 and 1824-25 and later presentations, by which time he had come to devote much less attention to the 'Oriental world'.

[23] Bernard McGrane, *Beyond anthropology: society and the Other* (New York: Columbia University Press, 1989) p. 94.

[24] Johannes Fabian, *Time and the Other: how anthropology makes its object* (New York: Columbia University Press, 1983) p. 26; McClintock, Imperial leather *op. cit.* pp. 40-42; my emphasis.

These oppositions are now commonplaces of postcolonial intellectual history – and in some measure are even reinscribed within postcolonialism itself – but they are, I think, unsatisfactory. I want to show that even at this most general level the absolutization of time and space turned on more than a binary rotation.

In the first place, 'anachronistic space' was riven by contradictory mappings. Within its confines, alterity could be conceived in two ways: the *excluded* other that could, at least in principle, be brought into the centre through incorporation or hybridization; or the *irreducible* other that had to be acknowledged as incommensurable and irrecuperable. The first of these invoked a discourse of rights, the second a discourse of limits.[25] The distinction is important because the very rules for mapping anachronistic space were thereby rendered peculiarly unstable. Both of these strategies entered into the constitution of the colonial order of things, but they did so in different ways and implied different intellectual and ethical orientations to the centrality of Europe.

In the second place, the possibility of different orientations implies that 'anachronistic space' was itself never singular. I think it is possible to plot the cardinal axes of this space of alterity, the effective matrix for the geographical imaginary of post-Enlightenment Europe, through a simple thought-experiment. This involves an elementary application of Greimas's semiotic square, and since this is a meaning-making machine with all sorts of limitations, I must emphasise the preliminary and propaedeutic nature of what follows. The origin (S) of this grid is 'Europe', which I will place in quotation marks throughout my discussion in order to accent its cultural constructedness or, more technically, its discursive constitution. It is this primary space, so to speak, that generates 'Asia' as a secondary space of opposition (–S) and 'Africa' as a tertiary space of contradiction ($\bar{\ }$S), both of which I will also mark to call attention to their discursive constitution (Figure 2).

I can make this clearer by outlining the logical operations through which those secondary and tertiary spaces are generated. K.N. Chaudhuri insists that the production of 'Asia' as a discursive category was 'essentially Western' and that 'there [was] no equivalent word in any Asian language nor such a concept in the domain of geographical knowledge.' He argues that:

> '[It] is the principle of non-contradiction that establishes the identity of Asia, even though its civilisations and people are markedly different from one another. Of course, besides being non-European, Asia is also non-African, non-American and so on. *There is a sequence of exclusions of which [being] non-European comes first.*' [26]

---

[25] Kalpana Seshadri-Crooks, 'At the margins of postcolonial studies', *Ariel* 26 (1995) pp. 47-71.

[26] K.N. Chaudhuri, *Asia before Europe: economy and civilisation of the Indian Ocean from the rise of Islam to 1750* (Cambridge: Cambridge University Press, 1990) pp. 22-3; my emphasis.

Similarly, Christopher Miller argues that within the Eurocentric discourse of Orientalism, 'the Orient' was constituted as

> 'a negative for Europe, conforming to the profile of what Europe thinks Europe is *not*; the opposition is therefore diametrical, producing a single, symmetrical Other. That Other always has a separate identity of its own, an "inferior" culture but a culture nonetheless, namely Islam. The negativity of Orientalism is that of a fully constituted nonself.'[27]

Miller goes on to argue that 'the two interlocking profiles of Europe and the Orient have no room for a third element, ['Africa'], endowed with a positive shape of its own.'[28]

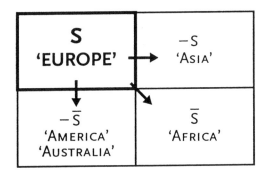

Figure 2

For Hegel, as is well known, 'Africa' was 'an unhistorical continent with no movement or development of its own.' Denied the vital presence of the modern state, Hegel claimed that historicity was necessarily absent – he thought that 'life there consists of a succession of contingent happenings and surprises' – which in turn meant that 'Africa' could be endowed with 'no subjectivity but merely a series of subjects who destroy one another.' Hence his infamous declaration that 'Africa', which had 'remained cut off from all contacts with the rest of the world', was 'the land of childhood, removed from the light of self-conscious history and wrapped in the dark mantle of night.'[29] It is not difficult to see how Miller can conclude from all this that, within the post-Enlightenment geographical imaginary, 'Africa' was constituted as 'the Other's Other, the Orient's Orient', 'an empty slate written on by

---

[27] Christopher Miller, *Blank darkness: Africanist discourse in French* (Chicago: University of Chicago Press, 1985) p. 15; for further discussion of French-language constructions of 'Africa', see T. Carlos Jacques, 'From savages and barbarians to primitives: Africa, social typologies and history in eighteenth-century French philosophy', *History and Theory* 36 (1997) pp. 190-215.

[28] Miller, Blank darkness *op. cit.*, p. 16.

[29] Hegel, History *op. cit.*, pp. 174, 176, 190.

outsiders.' European desire 'projects onto Africa a monstrous impossibility whose only existence is on paper', he writes: the continent emerges as a 'blank darkness' which, through its inscription of contradiction, calls into question 'the very terms and conditions of the discourse that created it.'[30]

What about the fourth quadrant, the space that in Greimas's original formulation was neither proscribed nor abnormal ($-\bar{\text{S}}$), 'the impossible space' that was supposed to destabilise the operation of the whole system? For Hegel this space was the New World of Australia and America, which was 'new', so he said, 'by virtue of its wholly peculiar character in both physical and political respects'. Hegel's own treatment of Australia was perfunctory, but modern scholars have identified a 'myth of antipodality', a 'phantasm' in which 'Australia' was seen as both 'a repository of all that is perverse, odd, unexpected' and as a locus that disclosed not only European desire but also European anxiety.[31] Be that as it may, Hegel was much more aware of the radical significance of 'America' for his philosophy of world history:

> 'America is the country of the future, and its world-historical importance has yet to be revealed in the ages which lie ahead.... It is a land of desire for all those who are weary of the historical arsenal of old Europe.... It is up to America to abandon the ground on which world history has hitherto been enacted. What has taken place there up to now is but an echo of the Old World and the expression of an alien life; and as a country of the future, it is of no interest to us here...'[32]

I don't want to claim very much for this exercise, which I know needs to be qualified in all sorts of ways, but it does allow me to draw three conclusions.

In the first place, mapping the production of meaning as a semiotic square shows how the post-Enlightenment geographical imaginary could be constructed in such a way *that 'Europe' was constituted as the locus from which sovereign meaning was to be endowed.* This, I assume, is the (produced) position of 'Europe-as-Subject'.

In the second place, the semiotic square shows *that the production of imaginative geographies was articulated within a system of difference.* Journals, maps, inventories and gazetteers were all quite literally lines in the articulation of a system of difference, 'forms of spatial punctuation' as Paul Carter calls them, which not only transformed

---

[30] Miller, Blank darkness *op. cit.*, p. 16; Miller's phrase mimics Hegel's 'dark mantle of night' but it also deliberately evokes Joseph Conrad's *Heart of Darkness*, in which Marlow recalls his childhood desire to explore central Africa, 'the biggest, the most blank' space on the Victorian map: 'It had got filled since my boyhood with rivers and lakes and names. It had ceased to be a blank space of delightful mystery – a white patch for a boy to dream gloriously over. It had become a place of darkness.' For other views, see V.Y. Mudimbe, *The invention of Africa* (Bloomington: Indiana University Press, 1988) and idem, *The idea of Africa* (Bloomington: Indiana University Press, 1994).

[31] Ryan, Cartographic eye *op. cit.*, p. 10; Ross Gibson, *South of the West: postcolonialism and the narrative construction of Australia* (Bloomington: Indiana University Press, 1992) p. x.

[32] Hegel, History *op. cit.*, pp. 171.

space into an object of knowledge – 'something that could be explored and read' – but which also made it possible for the particularity of place to be called into presence, brought within a European horizon of meaning, by positioning it within a grid of absences.[33] If the spaces in the grid were co-dependent, it does not follow that the relationships between them were as clear, as stable or even as systematic as my simple thought-experiment requires. But they were, none the less, in their lability and ambiguity, capable of significantly affecting one another.

In the third place, *these discursive productions were never direct, fully-formed and all-powerful projections from metropolitan cultures.* There was a hierarchy of interlocking circuits through which these various presuppositions and representations moved, in the course of which many of them were reworked, called into question, abandoned and, on occasion, reinstated. No doubt Europeans journeyed through Africa with cultural baggage that provided them with a generalised map of the landscape: the 'Dark Continent', say. But most of them also recognised the concrete and corporeal specificity of their experiences – the Sudan was not the Congo, after all – and modified their understandings in the light of their travels.[34] This has two consequences. On the one side, we need to allow for degrees of empirical adequacy: imaginative geographies were fabrications – all representations are – but this does not make them fictions, and it is foolish to claim that they reveal only the preconceptions and preoccupations of Europe. It is equally wrong-headed for any of us to adopt the superior position of 'monarch-of-all-I-survey' gazing out over a vast continent of misrepresentation: this is merely to 'other' those who were doing the 'othering'.[35] On the other side, however, we also need to allow for the indeterminacy of those representations. What seemed plausible in the lecture hall of the Royal Geographical Society in London, for example, might well become a half-truth on the ground. As imaginative geographies were circulated from field to library and back again, they passed through different sites of knowledge production that were connected in ramifying networks of exchange, and they inevitably interpenetrated, confounded and reworked one another. The hierarchical organisation of these networks was uneven and unstable, and if institutions in Europe's capital cities were powerful 'centres of calculation', as Bruno Latour calls them, critical points through which all nineteenth-century knowledges had to pass for legitimation and accumulation, nevertheless those

---

[33] Paul Carter, *The road to Botany Bay: an essay in spatial history* (London: Faber, 1987).

[34] Cf. Patrick Brantlinger, 'The genealogy of the myth of the "Dark Continent"', in his *Rule of darkness: British literature and imperialism, 1830-1914* (Ithaca: Cornell University Press, 1988).

[35] Cf. James Duncan, 'Sites of representation: place, time and the discourse of the Other', in James Duncan and David Ley (eds.) *Place/culture/representation* (London and New York: Routledge, 1993) pp. 39-56.

capital sites never fully succeeded in bringing the rest of the world under effective surveillance from the metropolis.[36]

I do not mean to trace the successive transformations of the semiotic square down to our own present; I doubt that it would survive the journey. It is of course the case that the post-Enlightenment geographical imaginary has been transformed in the course of the twentieth century, not least through the emergence of 'America' as the dominant habitus of 'the West' and, much later, by the disruptive colonization of 'Western' modernity by what some commentators see as a distinctively 'Asian' modernity: hence the appearance of a sort of 'Techno-Orientalism' or 'Japan panic' and its strange obverse, an alternative modernity whose 'Confucianism' often turns out to be fully conformable with the ideology of global capitalism.[37] But I strongly suspect that the absolutization of time and space continues to occupy a central place within the discourse of (post) modernity and that the semiotic square that I have presented here continues to figure, at least in spectral form, in the persistent search for narrative mastery.[38]

Exhibiting the world

World exhibitions first appeared in the middle of the nineteenth century, and it has since become a commonplace to treat them as exemplary sites of capitalist modernity. From their very beginning they were 'sites of pilgrimages to the commodity fetish', as Walter Benjamin once memorably remarked, and the early exhibitions were dominated by the new products and powers of industrial capitalism in Europe and North America. These displays were instrumental in expanding the boundaries of an exuberant commodity culture, but the world exhibitions also re-worked an aesthetic of collecting that could be traced back to the eighteenth-century

---

[36] Bruno Latour, 'Centres of calculation', in his *Science in action* (Milton Keynes, UK: Open University Press, 1987) pp. 215-257; see also David Philip Miller, 'Joseph Banks, empire, and "centers of calculation" in late Hanoverian London', in David Philip Miller and Peter Hanns Reill, *Visions of empire: voyages, botany and representations of nature* (Cambridge UK: Cambridge University Press, 1996) pp. 21-37.

[37] David Morley and Kevin Robins, 'Techno-Orientalism: Japan panic', in *Spaces of identity: global media, electronic landscapes and cultural boundaries* (London: Routledge, 1995) pp. 147-173.

[38] I take this latter phrase from Kerwin Klein. 'We have foresworn Hegelian hubris and created new forms for narrating postcolonial histories of cultural change,' he writes, 'but that deep antinomy remains, surfacing unbidden at inopportune moments and wreaking havoc on our attempts to understand the global world in which we live.' See Kerwin Lee Klein, 'In search of narrative mastery: postmodernism and the people without history', *History and Theory* 34 (1995) pp. 275-298. On the absolutism of Hegel's schema and its successor projects, see also Fernando Coronil, 'Beyond Occidentalism: toward nonimperial geohistorical categories', *Cultural Anthropology* 11 (1996) pp. 51-87.

cabinet of curiosities. It is the articulation of these two modalities of display, the conjunction of emporium and empire, that I want to emphasise here.

By the closing decades of the nineteenth century world exhibitions inscribed a double mapping. On one side they produced a space that traced in material and usually monumental form the movement of Reason, an evolutionary narrative of progress in which white mythology was made visible and celebrated as technological triumph. On the other side they produced a space increasingly given over to 'a parodic counterdisplay of the exotic', a liminal space of un-Reason, filled with a 'narcotic jumble of images' from other, colonised cultures that offered a hallucinatory glimpse into a world which, if it threatened never quite overwhelmed the poetics of imperial perspective.[39] Through this double mapping, world exhibitions provided a dramatic condensation of the post-Enlightenment geographical imaginary. I want to argue that this was made possible through a series of strategies which, far from being confined to the exhibition – or the museum and the zoo, those other icons of nineteenth-century Europe's culture of display – was constitutive of colonial modernity at large. The world exhibition brings these strategies of representation into view with such clarity that I begin my account there, but I will then spiral away from its grounds and enclosures. The focus of my account is the formation of what John Rajchman calls 'a space of constructed visibility'.[40] There were of course many such spaces, but I confine myself to four characterizations of the world exhibitions.

First, unlike those earlier cabinets of wonders, the exotic objects displayed at the world exhibitions were seen not as singular – 'rare, uncommon and even unthought creations' – but as *representative* of places in a larger system of order. This representative function mattered because it made the whole world metonymically present, and in the course of the nineteenth and early twentieth centuries the density of these displays was intensified through the proliferation of networks of objects, buildings and eventually people that steadily brought ever more exotic 'places' inside an ever more totalizing metropolitan 'gazeteer'.[41]

---

[39] Meg Armstrong, '"A jumble of foreignness": the sublime musayums of nineteenth-century fairs and expositions', *Cultural Critique* (1992-3) pp. 199-250; Curtis Hinsley, 'Strolling through the colonies', in Michael Steinberg (ed.) *Walter Benjamin and the demands of history* (Ithaca: Cornell University Press, 1996) pp. 119-140. Invoking the poetics of imperial perspective ought not to blind us to the tension between nation-centred and transnational exhibitionary orders; national rivalries were scarcely foreign to world exhibitions, but the important point here is the distinction between the 'space of Reason', within which European and North American nations displayed their antagonisms and differences (and jostled for position), and the 'space of un-Reason' within which other cultures were put on display.

[40] John Rajchman, 'Foucault's art of seeing', in his *Philosophical events: essays of the 80s* (New York: Columbia University Press, 1991) pp. 68-102.

[41] Carol Breckenridge, 'The aesthetics and politics of colonial collecting: India at world fairs', *Comparative Studies in Society and History* 31 (1989) pp. 195-216; Susan Stewart, *On longing: narratives of the miniature, the gigantic, the souvenir, the collection* (Durham: Duke University Press, 1984) p. 162;

Second, this ordering of things imagined the world as a *transparent* space: fully visible, exhaustively surveyable and so completely knowable. Its realization depended on the construction of a 'super-vision machine', a technology of representation that is also a technology of desire, in which the world exhibition becomes 'the panorama of panoramas', offering the tantalising prospect of 'a distant reality that can be possessed, that is always on the verge of being annexed or colonised.' This cultural formation installs a profoundly phallocentric economy of meaning whose artifice is concealed by the very transparency of its scenography: 'by establishing a distance which separates the object from the subject, the self from the scene, by being a "non-place".'[42]

Third, this representation of space was profoundly *public*, in the sense of both 'ordering objects for public inspection' and 'ordering the public that inspected.' The new exhibitionary complex produced a space within which the metropolitan public was constituted as the collective *subject* of knowledge, at once anonymous and yet indelibly marked with the sign of Europe, and hence engaged with the project of colonial modernity. To be sure, reception was varied and sometimes even critical. Colonial subjects visiting the world exhibitions were ambiguous in their responses too, sometimes identifying with the imperial project and at others parrying the 'spectacular gestures' of imperial culture by identifying themselves as 'seeing subjects at the heart of empire.' But it is the field within which these subject-positions were constituted – the site of spectatorship – which is the heart of the matter. Occupying a privileged vantage point, this new public was 'inveigled into complicity' with the dominant system of power-knowledge 'rather than cowed into submission before it.'[43]

Fourth, this rhetoric of complicity depended on an architecture of the gaze that was inherently *domesticating*. This was true not only in the sense that exhibitions were dreamworlds – 'cities of dreams within cities of painful actuality', attractions that distracted metropolitan eyes from the shock of capitalist modernity at home [44] – but also in the sense that their parodic versions of the urban re-presented the unfamiliar

---

Tony Bennett, *The birth of the museum: history, theory, politics* (London and New York: Routledge, 1995) pp. 84, 213.

[42] Lieven de Cauter, 'The panoramic ecstasy: on world exhibitions and the disintegration of experience', *Theory, Culture and Society* 10 (1993) pp. 1-23; Gillian Rose, 'Distance, surface, elsewhere: a feminist critique of the space of phallocentric self/knowledge', *Environment and Planning D: Society & Space* 13 (1995) pp. 761-781. This super-vision machine had a geopolitical as well as a cultural dimension, which I consider in the next section.

[43] Bennett, Birth of the museum *op. cit.*, p. 67; Antoinette Burton, 'Making a spectacle of empire: Indian travellers in fin-de-siècle London', *History Workshop Journal* 42 (1996) pp. 126-146.

[44] This has been a stock-in-trade of cultural criticism since Benjamin; for a particularly vivid elucidation of this theme, see Allan Pred, *Recognizing European modernities: a montage of the present* (London and New York: Routledge, 1995).

within the familiar forms of arcades, commercial streets and city promenades. What Herman Lebovics calls 'the seductions of the picturesque' rendered the violence of colonial appropriation all but invisible. In staging the world as an exhibition, then, aesthetic appreciation was transformed into political ontology. The colonial order of things was detached and distanced from its concrete particularities, compartmentalized and serialized. It was glossed as a harmonious visual composition and its more disturbing pathologies placed under erasure: 'a non-Western civilization that can be approached by subway, picnic basket in hand' loses much of its power to disconcert.[45]

It should be clear from these summary characterizations that the world exhibition was not only a space produced to make objects visible in particular ways; it was also a space in which – *and by means of which* – claims to knowledge were negotiated and legitimated. If the world exhibition was the materialization of an epistemological space, however, this was not the only topography within which European thought moved. Still less was it secure.[46] These are necessary cautions, but they do not blunt the colonising power constituted through this kind of epistemological space. Indeed, the production of an enframed totality is focal to Timothy Mitchell's account of what he calls 'the world-as-exhibition'. He argues that by the closing decades of the nineteenth century it had become a characteristic of European ways of knowing to render things as objects to be viewed: to 'set the world up as a picture [and arrange] it before an audience as an object on display, to be viewed, experienced and investigated.' Within this optic, the certainty of representation which is the guarantee of truth turns on the establishment of a distance between the observer and observed. From that position order may be dis-covered and re-presented. As Mitchell explains:

---

[45] Herman Lebovics, 'The seductions of the picturesque and the irresistible magic of art', in *True France: the wars over cultural identity, 1900-1945* (Ithaca: Cornell University Press, 1992) pp. 51-97.

[46] This is a matter whose complexity I can most readily convey through T.J. Clark's reading of Manet's *Exposition Universelle de 1867*. He sees this as a deliberately parodic rendering of conventional attempts to represent the modern city – and by extension what he calls 'the city containing the world' – as a legible totality. To Clark, the spectators in the foreground of the painting are 'transparent citizens' who want and expect Paris to be spread out in front of them 'like a gas-lit picture in a diorama.' Hence 'everything is held in place by vision and design'; the view is 'focussed and framed as a unity for the man in binoculars', but Clark says it might as well be that of the balloonist who is suspended awkwardly in the upper right of the frame. And yet the effect of the painting, so he argues, is to emphasise 'the artifice involved in having a city thus available to vision.' Both the composition and the brush-work imply that the canvas is 'not quite a picture, not quite finished.' There is thus a more general sense in which the totality constantly exceeds its representation, a sense in which, as Christopher Prendergast suggests, its closures are forever interrupted and prised open, so that, at the limit, 'the visible comes to *be* the illegible.' See T.J. Clark, 'The view from Notre-Dame', in his *The painting of modern life: Paris in the art of Manet and his followers* (Princeton: Princeton University Press, 1984) especially pp. 61-6; Christopher Prendergast, 'The high view: three cityscapes', in his *Paris and the nineteenth century* (Oxford UK and Cambridge MA: Blackwell, 1992) pp. 46-73.

'Without a separation of the self from a picture ... it becomes impossible to grasp "the whole". The experience of the world as a picture set up before a subject is linked to the unusual conception of the world as an enframed totality, something that forms a structure or system.'

What makes such a conception so unusual is that the process of enframing on which it relies conjures up a framework that seems to exist apart from, and prior to, the objects it contains – a framework that appears 'as order itself, conceived in no other terms than the ordering of what was orderless, the coordinating of what was discontinuous.' This is a highly particular way of thinking about – and indeed being in – the world, so Mitchell argues, which is peculiar to European modernity.[47]

This apparatus is colonising because it revolves around the power to represent conferred by its distinction between 'representation' and 'reality'. On the one side is representation: mounted from and staged within the space of the world-as-exhibition, its horizon of possibility is mapped, literally so, by the positivity of what Heidegger called the 'ground plan', the *Grundrisse*, from which the subject derives meaning, coherence, order. On the other side is 'reality': formed by 'the things-in-themselves', it is 'a pristine realm existing prior to all representation', 'an external realm of pure existence', distinguished by an essential absence (the ground plan). Within this framework order not only becomes visible in opposition to the disorder of things: it is made to appear through its traverse from outside. It is through the production of a space of constructed visibility – through the practices that produce and sustain its extensions and incursions in what Mitchell describes as an extended 'sequence of exhibitions' – that the world is made open to a colonising 'objectivity' that sanctions imperial measurement and regulation.[48]

Describing the world-as-exhibition as an epistemological space does not contract critical discussion to the philosophical-theoretical, since there are multiple passages that thread in and out of other cultural registers. When Benjamin claimed that the fin-de-siècle drawing room cluttered with memorabilia and curios, many of them from Europe's colonies, continued to provide 'a box in the world theatre', he was I think recognising that the bourgeois interior gave out onto the panoramic vision of a much wider visual culture and its dominant representations of space. And when Mary Louise Pratt describes the 'monarch-of-all-I-survey' scene characteristic of so many Victorian accounts of exploration and travel as a central tropos of 'imperial stylistics', of the ways in which 'imperial eyes' produced the extra-European world for

---

[47] Timothy Mitchell, *Colonising Egypt* (Cambridge: Cambridge University Press, 1988) pp. 6-7, 22, 38; idem, 'Orientalism and the exhibitionary order', in Nicholas Dirks (ed.), *Colonialism and culture* (Ann Arbor: University of Michigan Press, 1992) pp. 290-317; quotation from p. 304.

[48] Mitchell, Colonising Egypt *op. cit.*, pp. 10, 21, 29; idem, 'Orientalism' *op. cit.*, pp. 301, 312.

metropolitan European publics, she is in effect acknowledging that it trades on and reproduces the epistemological space of the world-as-exhibition.[49]

Let me illustrate what I mean by considering, very briefly, travel and travel-writing. During the nineteenth century, travel-writing moved in concert with the projects of natural history, and their formalization as a natural science was achieved through the production of a network of colonial and metropolitan spaces. Claims to knowledge made by these projects plainly depended on field work, on travels through what Dorinda Outram calls the 'wide open spaces of nature', but she shows that they were also inseparable from the production of the enclosed spaces of botanical gardens, museums and zoos. These spaces privileged not the corporeal passage of the traveller but the disembodied gaze of the scientist. Hence Cuvier held that 'true knowledge of the order of nature comes not from the whole-body experience of crossing the terrain', which provided 'little overview of the natural order as a whole', but from the very fact of the observer's distance from the field which alone made possible a properly 'panoramic' view. Nature was thus constituted as a space of closure uniquely accessible to a European public.[50]

In addition, there were close affinities between travel-writing and the development of the human sciences which were secured through common ethnographic descriptions and typifications. More revealing still, I think, though closely connected, are the filiations between the rise of international tourism and the popularization of anthropology. In nineteenth-century Europe, Mitchell notes, 'ordinary people were learning to live as tourists or anthropologists.' [51] Both of these positions required the development of strategies for visually comprehending – for sightseeing and exhibiting – other cultures which were read as coherent pictures or intelligible texts. These in turn depended on the production of networks that constituted a sort of double geography by means of which observation and detachment could be articulated. Thus European tourists venturing to Egypt were simultaneously assured that the traditional Orient was still available to their fascinated gaze, and reassured that they could safely inspect it from the viewing platforms of a recognisably 'European' modernity: grand hotels, restaurants, railway trains and river steamers. As Alvan Southworth, Secretary of the American Geographical Society, observed in 1874-5:

---

[49] Mary Louise Pratt, *Imperial eyes: travel writing and transculturation* (London and New York: Routledge, 1992) pp. 201-221.

[50] Dorinda Outram, 'New spaces in natural history', in N. Jardine, J.A. Secord and E.C. Spary (eds.) *Cultures of natural history* (Cambridge: Cambridge University Press, 1996) pp. 249-265.

[51] Mitchell, Colonising Egypt *op. cit.*, p. 28; see also Ellen Strain, 'Exotic bodies, distant landscapes: touristic viewing and popularized anthropology in the nineteenth century', *Wide Angle* 18 (1996) pp. 71-100; James Buzard, *The beaten track: European tourism, literature and the ways to "culture" 1800-1918* (Oxford: Clarendon Press, 1993).

'There is no country in the world that can be so completely inspected by the traveller. Not a square acre escapes your observation as you ascend the Nile to Khartoum and sail along its delta branches to Alexandria, Rosetta and Damietta... The book is before you. You only have to read the first page at Alexandria and turn over leaf after leaf as you linger by the cities... This is what makes the Nile travel so desirable. Amid luxury and fine companions you can leisurely examine all that the land contains...'

He was not alone. G.W. Steevens, a journalist with the *Daily Mail*, recalled with evident pleasure his trip on Thomas Cook's Nile steam-boat *Rameses the Great* . 'A vision of half-barbarous life passes before you all day,' he wrote, 'and you survey it in the intervals of French cooking.... Rural Egypt at Kodak range – and you sitting in a long chair to look at it.'[52]

At the end of our own century 'exhibiting the world' can call upon a much wider range of politico-visual technologies, but I don't propose to consider the ways in which these protocols reappear in and are reworked by contemporary cinema and video, travel and tourism, or a host of other cultural practices. Yet I do think that 'theory' is also a space of constructed visibility, with its own material supports, allowing the world to be seen in determinate and partial ways. And while other theoretical practices are possible – the reclamation of embodied vision through situated knowledges and the elaboration of non-representational theory among them[53] – I also believe that the discursive practices involved in 'exhibiting the world' remain continuous with the dominant protocols of much of our theorizing.

Normalizing the subject

Stoddart's vision of geography as a European science is founded on the extension of methods of observation, classification and comparison – the methods of natural history and natural science – 'to peoples and societies.' This allows him to posit a common space for both physical geography and human geography, but I want to complicate this claim in two ways. In the first place, I want to call into question any simple 'extension' by invoking Foucault's discontinuity between the eighteenth-century French 'classical' and the nineteenth-century French 'modern'. Foucault argues that the transition from one to the other was secured through the emergence of an anonymous, polymorphous and capillary power which established the groundwork for what he calls a 'society of normalization' and, with it, the formation of the

---

[52] See my 'Scripting Egypt: Orientalism and the cultures of travel', forthcoming in James Duncan and Derek Gregory (eds.) *Writes of passage* (London and New York: Routledge, 1998).

[53] See Donna Haraway, 'Situated knowledges: the science question in feminism and the privilege of partial perspective', in her *Simians, cyborgs and women: the reinvention of nature* (London and New York: Routledge, 1991) pp. 183-201; Nigel Thrift, '"Strange country": meaning, use and style in non-representational theories', in his *Spatial formations* (London: Sage, 1996) pp. 1-50.

human sciences. His construction of this new, disciplinary power mimics the space of Stoddart's intellectual cartography with remarkable fidelity: it is 'exercised by surveillance rather than ceremonies, by observation rather than commemorative accounts, by comparative measures that have the "norm" as reference.' But precisely because he moves beyond a narrowly epistemological horizon Foucault is able to map an altogether different space, one in which power-knowledge enters deeply into the constitution of human subjectivities. In the second place, however, Foucault's account was modelled on the transition from the Ancien Régime to post-revolutionary France: 'The "Enlightenment",' he declares, 'which discovered the liberties, also invented the disciplines.' The Enlightenment was not confined to Europe, of course, and Foucault suggested that his examples could indeed have been drawn from the sites of colonialism; but he himself never considered these issues, and in fact I will also want to call into question any simple 'extension' of disciplinary power from metropolitan to colonial societies.[54]

I cannot hope to reproduce the intricacy of Foucault's genealogy of normalization here, and I will simply note three moments in its formation. First, Foucault believed that normalization had its origins in the production and proliferation of binary distinctions: it depended on conceptual pairings of 'presence' and 'absence' in which the first term was valorized and the second term was marginalized. In Foucault's eyes, modern societies were discursively constituted through a series of normalizing judgements that were put into effect by a system of divisions and oppositions. He traced this process in his histories of the clinic, madness, the prison, and sexuality, so that Europeans came to constitute themselves as (for example) rational subjects by producing boundaries between themselves and those construed as insane. If this is a generalized strategy of Western metaphysics, its materialization involved the installation of geographies of partition: the production of spaces of purification and spaces of exclusion.

Second, Foucault argued that the spaces of exclusion were segmented and serialized. They were marked through a network of instruments and institutions for measuring, classifying, comparing and supervising. These various techniques made up the 'disciplines', and Foucault claimed that they worked through 'a political anatomy of detail' that superimposed two grids over the population. One grid lowered what he called 'the threshold of describable individuality' far below the summit of sovereign power – below the figures of monarchs, emperors, judges and generals – with the result that the bodies and lives of ordinary men and women were *objectified* by being turned into writing; they were nominated and en-listed as 'calculable' individuals within the apparatus of disciplinary power. The other grid

---

[54] Michel Foucault, *Discipline and punish: the birth of the prison* (London: Penguin, 1979) pp. 193, 222, 314n.

inaugurated a systematic surveillance – what Foucault, invoking Bentham, termed a 'panopticism' – through the production of 'so many small theatres, in which each actor is alone, perfectly individualized and constantly visible', with the result that they were also *subjectified* as the bearers of disciplinary power:

> 'He who is subjected to a field of visibility, and who knows it, assumes responsibility for the constraints of power; he makes them play spontaneously upon himself; he inscribes in himself the power relation in which he simultaneously plays both roles; he becomes the principle of his own subjection.'[55]

Third, Foucault suggested that disciplinary power began its work in enclosed institutions like barracks, schools and workshops, but that the disciplines slowly and unevenly emerged from these peripheral locations. They became detached from spaces of exclusion and swarmed in towards the centre until, at the limit, they would punctuate the whole surface of society with centres of observation to constitute a 'disciplinary society' directed towards the production of 'useful individuals'.[56]

I regard these three claims as productive and provocative hypotheses, and I want to explore their implications for the constitution of an explicitly colonial modernity by advancing some hypotheses of my own.

I should say at once that colonialism produced many of its spaces of exclusion through the appropriation of land and territory backed by the exceptional violence of sovereign (not disciplinary) power. Such terrible and exemplary violence may have been exercised sporadically, but it cast long shadows over colonized societies. The modalities of power that rippled through these spaces of exclusion were connected to Foucault's 'history of detail', but they cannot be reduced to the graphical projections of a purely disciplinary power. Still, these appropriations found their legitimation in a colonial imaginary which, as I have already shown, was sustained by the systematic production of a grid of presences and absences in which 'Europe' as sovereign subject was both produced and valorized by its difference from 'Asia', 'Africa', and 'America'. Although Foucault himself drew attention to the Orient as being both 'offered to the colonising reason of the West, yet indefinitely inaccessible for it always remains the outer limit', he never elaborated on what he meant. But Said's remarkable critique of Orientalism can be read, at least in some measure, as an attempt to reconstruct the missing history of this 'great divide'.[57]

---

[55] Ibid., pp. 139, 191-3, 199, 200, 202-3, 219, 220.

[56] Ibid., pp. 209, 211, 217, 304.

[57] Edward Said, *Orientalism* (London: Penguin, 1978). I suggested at the outset that the intellectual relations between Said and Foucault are contentious, but I think them closer – in *Orientalism* at any rate – than has been recognised by those critics who are content to juxtapose a 'humanist' Said to an 'anti-humanist' Foucault: see Derek Gregory, 'Imaginative geographies', *Progress in Human Geography* 19 (1995) pp. 447-485.

It is through discursive processes of this kind that the categories of 'metropole' and 'colony', 'centre' and 'periphery', were called into being. Colonial networks of information circulation were clearly directed towards that 'uninterrupted work of writing [that] links the centre and periphery' which Foucault identified within metropolitan societies, and which was supposed to constitute them as 'centres of calculation' through which all knowledges had to pass. But the system was highly imperfect, as I've said, and one historian claims that colonial collections and enumerations, reports and surveys sustained what was really a fantasy of empire: 'a paper empire built on a series of flimsy pretexts that were always becoming texts', and which created 'the myth of a unified archive, holding together the vast and various parts of the Empire.' [58]

Metropolitan surveillance may have been imperfect, uneven and discontinuous, but there were always also colonial 'centres of calculation': indeed, the administrative focus of the East India Company at Calcutta during the Bengal Presidency was called the 'Writer's Buildings'. Colonial governments clearly had a direct interest in enumerating their subaltern populations, and in the case of India anthropologists and historians have described how the prose of 'cadastral control' – in which standardised and routinised methods of measurement, calculation, classification and notation were 'drilled into the minutest bodily techniques of [native] measurers' – prepared the ground for a prose of 'civilian control' that rendered Indian bodies into what Arjun Appadurai calls 'a vast categorical landscape' whose enumeration was, so he suggests, a way of 'normalizing the pathology of difference through which the Indian social body was represented.' Appadurai claims that this process linked the construction of India as 'a museum or zoo of differences' with the project of 'cleaning up the sleazy, flabby, frail, feminine, obsequious bodies of natives into clean, virile, muscular, moral and loyal bodies that could be moved into the subjectivities proper to colonialism.' [59] In instances like these, one does see a transition towards a distinctive colonial governmentality in Foucault's sense of the term, 'in which power comes to be directed at the destruction and reconstruction of colonial space so as to produce not so much extractive-effects on colonial bodies as governing-effects on colonial conduct.' [60]

And yet equally often the scope of disciplinary power was limited. In many colonial regimes the disciplines did not swarm away from the margins towards the centre, and disciplinary power remained confined to enclosed sites like prisons, schools or plantations. In many (perhaps most) instances colonized people were

---

[58] Foucault, Discipline *op. cit.*, p. 197; Thomas Richards, *The imperial archive: knowledge and the fantasy of empire* (London: Verso, 1993) pp. 4-6.

[59] Arjun Appadurai, 'Number in the colonial imagination', in his *Modernity at large: cultural dimensions of globalization* (Minneapolis: University of Minnesota Press, 1997) pp. 114-135.

[60] David Scott, 'Colonial governmentality', *Social Text* 43 (1995) pp. 191-220.

constituted primarily as the *objects* of colonial knowledge rather than its subjects. Colonial states relied on repressive power to such a degree that medical disciplines – for example – were much less central to colonial rule than they were in the modern European state, and their insistence on inspecting and touching colonial bodies – treating them not as sacred but as secular – was often the occasion of considerable resistance.[61] And enumeration was usually a preliminary to aggregation. This was the rule rather than the exception in all colonial societies, which were much less virulently individualising in their powers than the metropolitan states which were Foucault's concern. By the closing decades of the nineteenth century, for example, colonial knowledges no longer constructed India as a cultural landscape to be remade in the image of Britain; on the contrary, India was made known through categories that constituted it as fundamentally *different* from Europe, and most important was caste, which was seen to be visibly inscribed on the body of 'typical' members who were supposed to bear the 'essential characteristics' of the collective caste.[62]

I want to suggest that this obsession with typifications and stereotypes had as its corollary the direction of disciplinary power *at the normalization of resident white populations*. They were surely subject to a disciplinary gaze, which they 'brought to themselves' more or less as Foucault describes the process of 'subjectification'. Conduct books, household compendia, guidebooks and the like all helped to codify and consolidate the protocols and norms of white colonial society. This is not to say that they were direct and unmediated reflections of metropolitan cultures, and Anne Laura Stoler convincingly argues that European colonies were sites for 'new constructions of Europeanness' that were often at odds with metropolitan ones. So, for example, Benedict Anderson describes the white solidarities that 'linked colonial rulers from different national metropoles' as a 'tropical gothic' because they were bourgeois sensibilities that transposed, in grotesquely parodic form, the class solidarities of European aristocracies at home.[63]

These solidarities were inscribed in spatialities that dramatized the imaginative difference between colonizer and colonized. Thus Thomas Metcalf describes the fin-de-siècle elaboration of an 'ideology of distance' in colonial India, distinguished by

---

[61] Meaghan Vaughan, *Curing their ills: colonial power and African illness* (Cambridge UK: Polity Press, 1991); see also David Arnold, *Colonizing the body: state medicine and epidemic disease in nineteenth-century India* (Berkeley: University of California Press, 1993).

[62] Thomas Metcalf, *Ideologies of the Raj* (Cambridge UK: Cambridge University Press, 1994) pp. 43, 113.

[63] Anne Laura Stoler, 'Rethinking colonial categories: European communities and the boundaries of rule', in Dirks (ed.) Colonialism *op. cit.*, pp. 319-52; Benedict Anderson, *Imagined communities: reflections on the origin and spread of nationalism* (London: Verso, 1991; revised edition) pp. 152-3; see also Anne Laura Stoler, *Race and the education of desire: Foucault's History of sexuality and the colonial order of things* (Durham: Duke University Press, 1996) *op. cit.*, pp. 98-116.

the separate spaces of the bungalow residence, the civil lines, and the hill station.[64] Similar spatial ideologies can be identified, in displaced forms, in other colonial societies, and the settlement space of Anglo-India was not alone in being figured within what Gail Ching-Liang Low calls 'a topos of linearity and geometry':

> 'These geometric lines are not only literal descriptions of the physical settlement patterns of the European community, but are also vivid testimonies to the culture's persistent interest in demarcation, naming and segregation. The obsession with walls, detachment and spaces-in-between signals a fear, an imagined pressure from the "native quarters", whose bodily secretions and metaphorical productivity threaten to run riot and spill over established boundaries. Lines of demarcation were also lines of defence.'[65]

And yet the security provided by this distancing was always more apparent than real. This was in part a matter of day-to-day interaction. As Stoler argues more generally,

> 'The self-affirmation of white, middle-class colonials ... embodied a set of fundamental tensions between a culture of whiteness that cordoned itself off from the native world and a set of domestic arrangements and class distinctions among Europeans that produced cultural hybridities and sympathies that repeatedly transgressed these distinctions.'[66]

In part, however, these porosities were produced from within the discourse of normalization itself. Hence Low describes the 'other' side of Anderson's tropical gothic, in which 'other' spaces seemed to 'escape the panoptic surveillance of the male colonial eye as dark, inaccessible, feminised and veiled places of darkness':

> 'The language of the disciplinary and regulatory discourses produces an Other city which is always sinister, mysterious, and dark, and whose shadow always falls on the city of light. This Other, expressed through the nineteenth-century privilege of the body as transcoder of difference, always threatens to spill over the geometric divisions of the civilised body, oozing its contaminated bodily wastes, disgusting odours and noxious smells. It thrives under the sign of the ubiquitous body of the native which is forever invading hallowed ground.'[67]

'Paranoia fills palaces with hidden eyes.' And yet this very paranoia outlines the palpably brittle yet extraordinary power of normalization, so much so, indeed, that to Jane Jacobs 'the most permanent legacy of imperialism' is 'the contest between that which, through space itself, has been "naturalised" and that which has been made

---

[64] Metcalf, Ideologies *op. cit.*, pp. 177-185.

[65] Gail Ching-Liang Low, 'The city of dreadful night', in her *White skins, black masks: representation and colonialism* (London and New York: Routledge, 1996) pp. 156-190; quotation from p. 163.

[66] Stoler, Race *op. cit.*, p. 112.

[67] Low, 'The colonial uncanny', in White skins *op. cit.*, pp. 113-155; quotation from p. 149.

"illegitimate".' ⁶⁸ What is 'naturalised' – retrieved from the past as imperialist nostalgia and held out as prospect – is the subject of Europe.

David Slater has proposed a sort of countergeography to disrupt this normative history of the subject of Europe. In his view, one of the most unsettling ways in which we can learn from other regions, to interrupt and subvert the privileges Eurocentrism arrogates to itself, is by recognising that 'it is always the "marginal" or "peripheral" case which reveals that which does not immediately appear in what seem to be more *"normal"* cases.' ⁶⁹ I would prefer to argue that it is the very production of the categories of the normal and the marginal – centre and periphery – that needs to be called to account if we are to displace the privileges of Eurocentrism.

Abstracting culture and nature

Natural history, so Foucault tells us, occupied a 'regional' space within the classical *episteme* of eighteenth-century Europe, where it was constituted as part of a project to navigate the passage that had opened up between 'words' and 'things': 'to bring language as close as possible to the observing gaze, and the things observed as close as possible to words.' It was in some substantial sense a *mapping* of the order of nature, abstracting its various forms from what Pratt calls 'the tangled threads of their life surroundings' and locating them within a systematic taxonomy. This involved more than a European project of global order, however, in which its centres of calculation extended their networks into some of the (to them) remotest places on earth.

I say this because there is another sense in which, by this means, one sort of place was made to yield to another. Natural history 'dis-placed' its specimens, interrupting the ecological relations at particular places (which were seen as an array of sites), and then 're-placed' those specimens within the logical order of the table (which was seen as an array of sights). This imperative for Nature to be in its 'place', to be brought within the Space of Reason and there constituted as *itself* a 'space of closure', had considerable metaphorical force within the Enlightenment project of natural history. This continued to be the case as the classical gave way to the modern *episteme* – and as natural science replaced natural history – but I want to suggest that confining Nature to its proper 'place' assumed considerable metaphorical force within a much larger imaginative landscape.⁷⁰

---

⁶⁸ Jane Jacobs, *Edge of empire: postcolonialism and the city* (London and New York: Routledge, 1996) pp. 158-9.

⁶⁹ David Slater, 'On the borders of social theory: learning from other regions', *Environment and Planning D: Society & Space* 10 (1992) pp. 307-27.

⁷⁰ This paragraph draws on Foucault, Order of things *op. cit.*; Pratt, Imperial eyes *op. cit.*, p. 31; Gregory, Geographical imaginations *op. cit.*, pp. 21-26. On 'Nature' and the Space of Reason, see

In order to do so, I return to Hegel. He treated Nature as a foundation – a 'geographical basis' – for his philosophy of history:

> 'Man uses nature for his own ends; but where nature is too powerful it does not allow itself to be used as a means.... The torrid and frigid zones, as such, are not the theatre on which world history is enacted.... All in all, it is therefore the temperate zone which must furnish the theatre of history. And more specifically the northern part of the temperate zone....'[71]

These were not exceptional views in nineteenth-century Europe, and two discursive strategies were mobilised in accounts like them. The first involved the discrimination of nature. According to this view, pre-modern or non-modern cultures were at one with nature, intimately embedded in and even indistinguishable from their surrounding ecologies, whereas modern cultures were distinguished by their distance from and domination over nature. The second strategy involved the normalization of nature. According to this view, temperate nature was 'normal' nature; both the violence of intemperate nature, red in tooth and claw, and the siren song of a seductive and sultry tropical nature were safely distant from Europe in geological time or geographical space. For Hegel and his contemporaries, therefore, 'European man' was thus, *by his very nature*, not only 'modern man' but also 'normal man'.[72]

Both of these strategies invoked procedures of partition, exclusion and purification which Latour, following Foucault, takes to be intrinsic to the project – he would probably prefer to say the 'conceit' – of modernity and, his particular concern, its struggle to abstract 'culture' and 'nature'.[73] Latour's argument is compelling, but he does not pursue the predicaments occasioned by these procedures within *colonial* modernity. And there, as I want to show, these abstractions were much less secure than they seemed, at least on the surface, in Europe.

What happened when Hegel's 'European man' – the bearer of modern culture, 'civilization' – ventured into other Natures? In a short story called 'An outpost of progress', Joseph Conrad provided one typical answer. His protagonists were two agents of a trading company:

> 'They lived like blind men in a large room, aware only of what came in contact with them (and of that only imperfectly), but unable to see the general aspect of things. The river, the

---

Outram, 'New spaces' *op. cit.* and James Larson, *Reason and experience: the representation of natural order in the work of Carl von Linné* (Berkeley: University of California Press, 1971). I have taken the metaphoric of 'place' from the illuminating discussion in Charles Withers, 'Geography, Natural History and the eighteenth-century Enlightenment: putting the world in place', *History Workshop Journal* 39 (1995) pp. 137-163.

[71] Hegel, Lectures *op. cit.*, p. 155.

[72] See Derek Gregory, 'The geographical discourse of modernity', in *Explorations in critical human geography. Hettner-Lectures* 1 (Heidelberg: Department of Geography, 1998) pp. 45-67.

[73] Bruno Latour, *We have never been modern* (Cambridge MA: Harvard University Press, 1993).

forest, all the great land throbbing with life, were like a great emptiness. Even the brilliant sunshine disclosed nothing intelligible. Things appeared and disappeared before their eyes in an unconnected and aimless kind of way. The river seemed to come from nowhere and to flow nowhither. It flowed through a void.'

'Blind', 'unable to see the general aspect of things', this nature appeared to both men as 'a great emptiness', 'a void'. It was the oddest of natures, a Nature without a Space, where a river could come from nowhere and flow to nowhere. Later the hapless pair chance upon an old European newspaper containing an article on 'our colonial expansion':

'It spoke much of the rights and duties of civilisation, of the sacredness of the civilising work, and extolled the merits of those who went about bringing light, and faith, and commerce to the dark places of the earth. Carlier and Kayerts read, wondered and began to think better of themselves. Carlier said one evening, waving his hand about, "In a hundred years, there will perhaps be a town here. Quays, and warehouses, and barracks, and - and - billiard rooms. Civilization..."'[74]

Here at last was the prospect – literally so – of producing Space, of bringing Nature within the bounds of Reason. In these passages Conrad re-stages the metropolitan opposition between 'culture' and 'nature' as an opposition between a *colonial* culture and an *other* nature.

The same themes reappear five years later in his *Heart of Darkness*, where they are rendered with particular precision and economy. In this scene, Marlow has just arrived at one of the Company's trading stations in the Congo:

'When near the buildings I met a white man, in such an unexpected elegance of get-up that in the first moment I took him for a sort of vision. I saw a high starched collar, white cuffs, a light alpaca jacket, snowy trousers, a clear necktie, and varnished boots. No hat. Hair parted, brushed, oiled, under a green-lined parasol held in a big white hand. He was amazing, and had a penholder behind his ear.'

'I shook hands with this miracle, and I learned he was the Company's chief accountant....'

This extraordinary European figure presented a stark contrast to what Marlow sees as 'the great demoralization of the land' and the encroachments of its savage nature on the space of the trading station itself:

'Everything else in the station was in a muddle – heads, things, buildings. Strings of dusty niggers with splay feet arrived and departed; a stream of manufactured goods, rubbishy cottons, beads and brass-wire sent into the depths of darkness, and in return came a precious trickle of ivory.'

---

[74] Joseph Conrad, 'An outpost of progress', in *The complete short fiction of Joseph Conrad* (New York: Ecco Press, 1991) vol. 1; quotations from pp. 42-4; the story was first published in 1897.

'I had to wait in the station for ten days – an eternity. I lived in a hut in the yard, but to be out of the chaos I would sometimes get into the accountant's office ... [where], bent over his books, [the chief accountant] was making correct entries of perfectly correct transactions.'[75]

Marlow's overwhelming sense is one of disorder – the formless, brooding, indescribable jungle and even the seemingly arbitrary, inchoate activities of the Company itself – and yet, in the middle of all this, he glimpses (and seeks refuge in) a space of rationality, of calculability, the space of capital accounting.

Conrad's writings become commonplaces of postcolonial criticism, of course, and they have been subjected to radically discrepant readings, but these passages provide vivid illustrations of the European struggle to abstract 'culture' and 'nature' within the outliers of colonial modernity. What happens when the precarious geography of the trading station has been replaced by permanent colonial settlement?

We may take the two views of the 'native' city of Chandrapore with which E. M. Forster opens *A Passage to India* as exemplary:

'Edged rather than washed by the river Ganges, it trails for a couple of miles along the bank, scarcely distinguishable from the rubbish it deposits so freely.... The very wood [of the houses] seems made of mud, the inhabitants of mud moving. So abased, so monotonous is everything that meets the eye, that when the Ganges comes down it might be expected to wash the excrescence back into the soil. Houses do fall, people are drowned and left rotting, but the general outline of the town persists, swelling here, shrinking there, like some low but indestructible form of life.'

Inland, however, 'the prospect alters.' Viewed from the rise beyond the railway, where the European 'civil station' is laid out,

'Chandrapore appears to be a totally different place. It is a city of gardens. It is no city, but a forest sparsely scattered with huts. It is a tropical pleasaunce washed by a noble river. The toddy palms and neem trees and mangoes and pepul that were hidden behind the bazaars now become visible and in their turn hide the bazaars. They rise from the gardens where ancient tanks nourish them, they burst out of stifling purlieus and unconsidered temples. Seeking light and air, and endowed with more strength than man or his works, they soar above the lower deposit to greet one another with branches and beckoning leaves, and to build a city for the birds.'[76]

These two views are common motifs of the later colonial imaginary; they construct three sights/sites. In the first place, they set up two exhibitions of nature, two radically different images of what David Arnold has described as the profoundly ambivalent concept of 'tropicality'. One is an image of tropical nature as fallen,

---

[75] Joseph Conrad, *Heart of Darkness* (London: Penguin, 1985 edn.) pp. 45-7; the novella was first published in 1902.

[76] E.M. Forster, *A Passage to India* (London: Penguin, 1971 edn.) pp. 9-10; the novel was first published in 1924.

wretched and rotting – a nature of excrescence – and the other is an image of tropical nature as heterotopia, a prospect of delight and desire: a nature of abundance.[77] In the second place, these views enable Forster to assimilate colonized culture to tropical nature. Seen from within, the city of Chandrapore is part of a hideous, disfigured nature of excrescence. Seen from without, where the distance between the native city and the civil station is scrupulously established, the city can be recomposed as part of a nature of abundance. But Forster makes it clear that this is a powerful yet precarious fantasy: 'Newcomers cannot believe it to be as meagre as it is described, and have to be driven down to acquire disillusionment.'[78] In the third place, therefore, moving from one view to the other establishes an opposition between the culture of the colonizers and that of the colonized. The fantasy of a tropical heterotopia is possible only when the point of view is removed from the landscape, only when it is recognised that the civil station, with its regular geometry and its red-brick club on the brow, 'shares nothing with the city': which is all another way of saying that the civil station is *apart from* rather than *a part of* tropical nature.

Both Conrad and Forster suggest, in rather different ways, that these abstractions were highly unstable. Colonial cultures, with their fears of miscegenation and creolization, were also riven by fears of a different sort of hybridization. The colonial project required European culture to penetrate another nature, but there was also the dreadful possibility of reversal, of inversion, of another nature penetrating European culture. This is exactly how Michael Taussig, in a brilliantly disturbing reading, interprets the atrocities committed by agents of the Peruvian Amazon Company on the people of the Putamayo in the opening decade of our own century. At the time a committee of inquiry put the burden on the backs of political economy – on the capitalist logic of extracting low-grade rubber using scarce labour – but Taussig dismisses this economic 'rationalisation' as 'hallucinatory'. He suggests that the rubber traders feared a brute and animal nature which they saw surrounding them, advancing, threatening to engulf them, and which they identified with both the teeming darkness of the rainforest – an 'unnatural Nature' – and with the supposed savagery of the native people who lived in – who were part of – the rainforest: deviant creatures of a deviant Nature. Nature could not be contained within its proper place. And as the traders constructed this landscape of wildness and savagery,

---

[77] Arnold's central point is that 'we need to understand the tropics as a conceptual, and not just physical space': David Arnold, 'Inventing tropicality', in his *The problem of nature: environment, culture and European expansion* (Oxford UK and Cambridge MA: Blackwell, 1996) pp. 141-168; quotation from p. 142.

[78] Forster, Passage *op. cit.*, p. 10.

so they themselves became wild and savage: the violence of their actions mirrored the violence of their fears.[79]

Writing back

I have argued that the geo-graphs inscribed within the ideology of Eurocentrism underlabour to produce an abstract space. But in the course of its expansions, which are also erasures, 'Europe' has turned into 'the West' which, much more recently, has turned into 'the North'.[80] Each of these transitions is freighted with its own cultural baggage, of course, but their general burden is clear. As Edouard Glissant remarks, 'The West is not in the West. It is a project, not a place.'[81] It follows, I think, that 'Eurocentrism is not merely the ethnocentrism of people located in the West,' as Vivek Dhareshwar notes, but rather it 'permeates the cultural apparatus in which we participate.'[82] Our intellectual dispositions including, centrally, the theoretical attitude itself, cannot be immune from these cultural inscriptions. My own work has been marked by them, and – as I have constantly emphasised – we continue to inhabit the belly of the beast. That being so, let me return to where I started, the work of Edward Said, and repeat Gyan Prakash's verdict on its legacy:

> 'If "the West is now everywhere, within the West and outside", as Ashis Nandy suggests, then it is naive and politically self-defeating to expect a critique to arise from the "outside", from some supposed uncontaminated postcolonial experience. As Gayatri Chakravorty Spivak puts it, postcoloniality consists in catachrestic criticism that seizes the given apparatus to reverse and displace it; or in Homi Bhabha's terms, it is an in-between position of practice and negotiation. We would be missing the significance of *Orientalism* and the postcolonial critique it has inspired if, in the urge to place them in context, we overlook their catachrestic appropriation of Western theory derived from cross-hatching the histories of knowledge and imperialism. This has placed the empire at the very centre of Europe, deconstructing its self-same image. *Orientalism*'s subversive effect is derived from this postcolonial "writing back" it represents and has stimulated.'[83]

---

[79] Michael Taussig, *Shamanism, colonialism and the wild man* (Chicago: University of Chicago Press, 1987) esp. pp. 74-85.

[80] See, for example, the discussion in Christopher Gogwilt, *The invention of the West: Joseph Conrad and the double-mapping of Europe and Empire* (Stanford: Stanford University Press, 1995).

[81] Edouard Glissant, *Caribbean discourse: selected essays* (Charlotteville: University of Virginia Press, 1989) p. 2.

[82] Vivek Dhareshwar, 'The predicament of theory', in Martin Kreiswirth and Mark Cheetham (eds.), *Theory between the disciplines: authority/vision/politics* (Ann Arbor: University of Michigan Press, 1990) pp. 91-96; quotation is from p. 235.

[83] Gyan Prakash, 'Orientalism now', *History and Theory* 34 (1995) pp. 199-212.

This is the place to remind ourselves that geography is literally a kind of writing too: 'geo-graphing' or 'earth-writing'. Given the investments of this 'European science' in Eurocentrism, then it is surely time for us to join this 'writing back'.

THE GEOGRAPHICAL DISCOURSE
OF
MODERNITY

The geographical discourse of modernity*

DEREK GREGORY

Modernity, philosophy, geography

My title is, of course, borrowed from Jürgen Habermas. In those remarkable lectures which he delivered at the Collège de France in 1983 – lectures which were a *succès de scandale* in a Paris still mesmerised by Bataille, Derrida, Foucault and Lyotard – Habermas argued that the philosophical discourse of modernity begins with the legacy of Hegel. For Hegel was the first philosopher to conceive of modernity as a problem, and Habermas claimed that it is in his work that the 'constellation among modernity, time-consciousness and rationality becomes visible for the first time.'[1]

I want to begin with Hegel too, but I do so in order to advance a different set of arguments. For Hegel's legacy has been invested not only in conceptions of time but also in two other conceptions that appear, where they appear at all, in the very margins of Habermas's account: 'space' and 'nature'. These are equally vital moments in the constellation between modernity and rationality that so forcefully claimed Habermas's attention, and I want to suggest that they are equally indispensable terms not only for a genuinely human geography but also for a critical analysis of the turbulent world in which we live.

Asking which 'we' is always a good idea, however, and like several other commentators I am troubled by Habermas's profound Eurocentrism. So much of his work has been preoccupied with coming to terms with the history of twentieth-century Germany – with the redemption of the project of modernity in the face of the terrible and terrifying provocations of the Third Reich – that he has very little to say about the troubling legacy of quite other European empires and the formation of the extra-European world in which 'we' are all involved.[2] This enlarged horizon of

---

* This is a revised version of an address delivered at the University of Heidelberg on the occasion of the first Hettner-Lecture in June 1997. The argument is the same as that of my original presentation; I have clarified and corrected several passages and added the usual bibliographic apparatus. I should like to record my debt to Prof. Dr. Peter Meusburger, his colleagues and graduate students for their warm hospitality and engaging intellectual discussions throughout my stay in Heidelberg.
[1] Jürgen Habermas, *The philosophical discourse of modernity: twelve lectures* (Cambridge: Polity Press, 1987) (first published in German, 1985) p. 43.
[2] See Victor Li, 'Habermas and the ethnocentric discourse of modernity', in Martin Kreiswirth and Thomas Carmichael (eds.), *Constructive criticism: the human sciences in the age of theory* (Toronto: University of Toronto Press, 1995) pp. 44-58; Gerard Delanty, 'Habermas and Occidental

meaning transforms the very terms in which the project of modernity needs to be understood, both in the past and in the present, for it identifies a world in which, as James Clifford puts it, we are all 'caught between cultures, implicated in others.'[3] When Habermas objects to the ways in which the instrumental rationalities of the politico-economic system encroach upon the lifeworld, he describes this as a process of 'colonization': and yet he confines the term within the contours of Europe and North America, and his evolutionary schema remains strangely silent about the complicities between modernity and colonialism.[4] Exposing those connections involves uncovering a series of passages between the past and what I think of as the colonial present, and converts the project of modernity into something closer to the *predicament* of modernity, to borrow another of Clifford's phrases, in such a way that we are I think obliged to attend to its uneven and foliated geographies.

In making these claims, I should say at once that – although I am an historical geographer of sorts – I am not arguing in narrowly disciplinary terms. In the late twentieth-century academy, all disciplines have been drawn into a vigorous exchange of ideas and they have all opened themselves up to interdisciplinary, even post-disciplinary inquiry. In what has become quite literally a market-place of ideas, we are all now thieves, trespassers and magpies, taking home ideas we find on our travels. But we also leave signs of our presence in the language-games of other disciplines. One of the most extraordinary changes in the intellectual landscape that I inhabit – a change not merely in our maps of the landscape but in the very practice of mapping itself – has been the proliferation of ideas about 'space' and 'nature'. Their circulation across disciplinary frontiers has not only enriched my own discipline. It has also radically transformed the whole field of the humanities and the social sciences, which now attend to these questions with an unprecedented seriousness. And so I should like to raise two sets of closely connected questions, about 'space' and about 'nature', which bear directly on the interrogation of modernity.

Questions of space

The question of space is by no means foreign to Hegel, and I am hardly the first to identify its presence in his writings. Henri Lefebvre noted that within Hegelian

---

rationalism: the politics of identity, social learning and the cultural limits of moral universalism', *Sociological Theory* 15 (1997) pp. 30-59. Habermas is by no means alone in his Eurocentrism: see David Slater, 'On the borders of social theory: learning from other regions', *Environment and Planning D: Society & Space* 10 (1992) pp. 307-327.

[3] James Clifford, *The predicament of culture: twentieth-century ethnography, literature and art* (Cambridge MA: Harvard University Press, 1988) p. 11.

[4] Jürgen Habermas, *The theory of communicative action.* Vol. 2: *Lifeworld and system: a critique of functionalist reason* (Cambridge: Polity Press, 1987) (first published in German, 1985).

philosophy the movement of world-history was supposed to culminate in the modern state as what he called 'an immobile space which is the locus of realized Reason'. The identity between Space and Reason – between a particular spatiality and a particular rationality – is extremely suggestive, but the tragedy, Lefebvre believed, was that the subsequent critique of Hegel – including, centrally, that of Marx – involved not only the perfectly proper rejection of this 'fetishization of space' as a hideously fixed and frozen geometry, but also the much more problematic reaffirmation of time in such a way that it shattered what Lefebvre saw as 'the primacy of the spatial.' That is an awkward turn of phrase, however, because he went on to argue – I think correctly – that it was precisely the conjunction *between* productions of time and productions of space that marked 'the threshold of modernity'.[5]

Time, space and modernity

Whatever one makes of Lefebvre's particular theses, there can be no doubt that it has become commonplace to connect modernity to a changed consciousness of time. Many of its most influential critics work within a *cognitive-instrumental analytic* that is predisposed towards time as the measure of the modern. Thus modernity as discontinuity, a punctuation point in human history; modernity as velocity, an acceleration in the speed of social change; modernity as intensity, a transformation in the regimes of what the historian E.P. Thompson called 'time-discipline'.[6] All three motifs appear in Marx's critique of political economy, for example, where the construction of capitalism as a mode of production is made to revolve around time as embodied in labour, materialised in the commodity and appropriated as surplus value.

Other critics of modernity have emphasised an *aesthetic-affective analytic*, and many of them have given a central place to the poet Charles Baudelaire, whose essay on 'The painter of modern life' written in 1859-60 spoke of the need to capture 'the transient, the fleeting, the contingent'. Baudelaire's views of modernity were more complicated than this implies – he wanted to register the passing moment without destroying its passage, to recapture something eternal within the event itself – but it was none the less that fixation on time, a sense of restless animation, of a break with tradition, of a celebration of the *new*, that propelled a series of avant-garde movements through the

---

[5] Henri Lefebvre, *The production of space* (Oxford UK and Cambridge MA: Blackwell, 1991 (first published in French, 1978) pp. 21-2, 279; for further discussion, see Derek Gregory, 'Modernity and the production of space', in *Geographical imaginations* (Oxford UK and Cambridge MA: Blackwell, 1994) pp. 348-416.

[6] E.P. Thompson, 'Time, work-discipline and industrial capitalism', *Past & Present* 38 (1967) pp. 56-97.

nineteenth and into the early twentieth centuries.[7] Indeed, Habermas reminds us that the word 'avant-garde' entails 'invading unknown territory, exposing itself to the dangers of sudden, shocking encounters, conquering an as yet unoccupied future. The avant-garde must find a direction in a landscape into which no one seems to have yet ventured.'[8]

But this is an arresting passage. Unnoticed and unremarked, it has been taken over by another language: a metaphor of territory, occupation, landscape. I believe that this is indicative of a more general figuration of the modern. Within much of our critical discussion of modernity, if I may reverse a distinction drawn by Michel de Certeau, 'time' serves a strategic function – tracing the arc of the modern, the march of 'progress', the trajectory of 'take-off' – whereas 'space' constantly irrupts as a tactical displacement.[9]

In fact, modernism was never so silent about space as some supposedly postmodern commentators have claimed.[10] To return to the first of my examples, David Harvey has shown that Marx's critique of political economy, unlike the constitutively spaceless world of neoclassical economics, depends upon the formation of a *space-economy*: that capitalism requires the production and creative destruction of *landscapes* of capital accumulation. If Marx mapped capitalism as the Empire of Time, then we ought to recognise that the metaphor conveys an explicit spatialization – the *mapping* of an *empire* – whose analysis is indispensable to its critique.[11] Aesthetic modernism was always much less reticent in its explorations of spatial form and configuration and much more attentive to the possibilities of simultaneity and juxtaposition. Walter Benjamin's brilliant reading of Baudelaire, to revisit my second example, reveals a profound engagement by both authors with the fragmented and rationalized spaces of Hausmann's Paris, and most of all with the 'dialectics of seeing'

---

[7] Marshall Berman, 'Baudelaire: Modernism in the streets', in *All that is solid melts into air: the experience of modernity* (London: Verso, 1982) pp. 131-171; Christopher Prendergast, 'Baudelaire's watch: or the fast, the slow and the intelligible', in *Paris and the nineteenth century* (Oxford UK and Cambridge MA: Blackwell, 1992) pp. 189-214.

[8] Jürgen Habermas, 'Modernity versus postmodernity', *New German Critique* 22 (1981) pp. 3-14.

[9] Cf. Michel de Certeau, *The practice of everyday life* (Berkeley, CA: University of California Press, 1984) pp. 34-39.

[10] Cf. Edward Soja, *Postmodern geographies: the reassertion of space in critical social theory* (London: Verso, 1989); I elaborate this claim in Geographical imaginations *op. cit.*

[11] For a formal treatment of Marx and the political economy of space, see David Harvey, *The limits to capital* (Oxford UK and Cambridge MA: Blackwell, 1982); for Harvey's views on modernism and space, see his *The condition of postmodernity: an enquiry into the origins of cultural change* (Oxford UK and Cambridge MA: Blackwell, 1989).

– of spatializing – that were exemplified in that famous 'capital of the nineteenth century'.¹²

I want to suggest that tactical displacements of this order – these irruptions of the spatial – are vitally important to critical inquiry. As Michel Foucault once observed, the particular spaces of visibility that they produce – what Heidegger called the 'clearing' or *Lichtung,* the space in which and through which things are made visible to human thought in historically determinate ways – enable us 'to grasp precisely the points at which discourses are transformed in, through and on the basis of relations of *power.*' ¹³

Yet there is a reticence. And for this reason I think it still true to say, as Foucault did exactly twenty years ago, that 'a whole history remains to be written of spaces'.¹⁴ At that time my own discipline of geography was ill-equipped to undertake such a project. Many of its architects, at least in Britain and North America, were busily constructing a bridge between geography and geometry that would lead, so they hoped, to an autonomous science of the spatial. The history of this union between geography and geometry reminds me of the fairy-story in which the Prince kisses the frog and is immediately turned into another frog. For Foucault had gone on to say that such a history of spaces would also be 'a history of *powers*' (my emphasis); yet Anglo-American spatial science, unlike the German-language location theory on which it drew, was not only hostile to historical inquiry – its geometries spinning in an endless equilibrium – but it reduced the analysis of different forms of power to the purely technical calibration of different coefficients of the 'friction of distance'.¹⁵

Histories of space

Since then, the project of writing that richer history of space has involved both the socialization of geography and the spatialization of social theory. This joint project has been necessary in order to overcome the separation between 'society' and 'space'. This partition is, I think, actively unhelpful. It conjures up a busy world of institutions, interactions and practices on the one side ('society') that writes its collective signatures on the blank page that is the other side ('space'). The multiple senses in

---

¹² See Susan Buck-Morss, *The dialectics of seeing: Walter Benjamin and the Arcades Project* (Cambridge, MA: MIT Press, 1989); Margaret Cohen, *Profane illumination: Walter Benjamin and the Paris of surrealist revolution* (Berkeley, CA: University of California Press, 1993).

¹³ Michel Foucault, 'Questions on Geography', in his *Power/knowledge: selected interviews and other writings* (Brighton, UK: Harvester, 1980) pp. 63-77 (my emphasis). For a luminous elucidation of these issues, see John Rajchman, 'Foucault's art of seeing', in his *Philosophical events: essays of the 80s* (New York: Columbia University Press, 1991) pp. 68-102.

¹⁴ Michel Foucault, 'The eye of power', in his *Power/knowledge op. cit.,* pp. 146-165; this discussion was originally published in France in 1977.

¹⁵ See Eric Sheppard, 'Dissenting from spatial analysis', *Urban Geography* 16 (1995) pp. 283-303.

which social life *takes place* are thereby erased and the complex production of the spaces in which – and by *means* of which – we conduct our lives becomes lost from view.

The Swedish geographer Torsten Hägerstrand tells a marvellous story to illustrate the consequences of this state of affairs. One day, a little girl came home from school in tears. Her teacher had written three words on the blackboard – 'bear', 'tree' and 'mouse' – and asked the class to divide them into two groups. All her schoolfriends had put 'bear' and 'mouse' in one group and 'tree' in the other group, and the teacher was very pleased because this was the answer he had wanted. 'Science,' he had explained solemnly, 'depends on putting things into groups which have similar properties, because that is how we can make generalizations and predictions about them.' So 'bear' and 'mouse' belonged together: they were both animals. But the little girl had put 'bear' and 'tree' together because, as she explained tearfully to her mother, 'they are *found* together'. Her mother dried her daughter's eyes, thought for a moment, and then asked a question of her own: 'When you are walking through our forest, is it more important to know that bears are to be found among the trees; or would it be better, if you suddenly met a bear on the path, to say to yourself that *really* he's just like a mouse?'[16]

For a Canadian, this is still a good question. In fact, it was the basis for Kant's pivotal distinction between *logical* classifications that depend on similarity – on identity and difference – and *physical* classifications that depend on contiguity: 'finding things together'. Kant's lectures on physical geography, delivered at Königsberg between 1756 and 1796, made much of these physical classifications, which Kant saw as the distinctive foundations for both historical and geographical inquiry. I want to remove the divide that he proposed between the disciplines of history and geography, however, in order to make three observations about the history of space – which we might now think of as the history of 'finding things together'.

Geographies of time-space compression

First, the spaces in which things have been found together are highly variable. Perhaps the landscape of late eighteenth-century Europe was still a patchwork quilt of pockets, produced out of intensely local interactions between cultures and ecologies; perhaps the spaces of experience and the horizons of expectation of most men and women were still bounded by the familiar forms of farms and fields, by the church bell ringing through the village and the weekly journey to the market town. Perhaps: but surely not for Kant or Hegel. They knew that modern warfare had

---

[16] I have reworked the story from Nigel Thrift, 'Bear and mouse or bear and tree? Anthony Giddens's reconstitution of social theory', *Sociology* 19 (1985) pp. 609-23.

redrawn the map of Europe and changed the political economy of distance; they read the accounts of the naturalists and explorers who had brought back visions of a much wider world for a sophisticated European public; and they were keenly aware of the networks of European colonialism that reached around the globe.

Harvey has described these changes as a process of 'time-space compression'. The metaphor captures something of the sheer physicality of what is involved, the sense in which time and space seem to collapse inwards as our world becomes smaller. But Harvey wants to emphasise what he sees as the sense of *disorientation* produced by these changes, and cites the poet Heinrich Heine, who confessed to a 'tremendous foreboding' at the opening of the railway from Paris to Rouen and Orléans in 1843:

> 'What changes must now occur, in our way of looking at things.... Even the elementary concepts of time and space have begun to vacillate. Space is killed by the railways, and we are left with time alone.... Just imagine what will happen when the lines to Belgium and Germany are completed and connected up with their railways! I feel as if the mountains and forests of all countries were advancing on Paris. Even now, I can smell the German linden trees; the North Sea's breakers are rolling against my shore.'

Marx used the same image – 'the annihilation of space by time' – which was a leitmotif of the discourses of modernity in nineteenth-century Europe.[17]

But it is, I think, thoroughly deceptive. For time-space compression is a jagged and uneven process. Not only does it vary over time: it also has its own geographies.[18] Let me offer just one example, drawn from my own work on the global circulation of information in the nineteenth century. Habermas's discussion of the public sphere was limited to the nation-state, but the success of European colonialism and imperialism depended upon the construction of a *trans*national public sphere.[19] When the British Empire was at its height, nominally public information – 'nominally' because access to information was socially circumscribed in all sorts of ways – flowed unevenly and sporadically through overlapping and disjointed networks of railways, sailing ships, steamships, and telegraph lines, and crept slowly and uncertainly over mountains, across deserts and through rainforests. Certainly,

---

[17] David Harvey, 'Between space and time: reflections on the geographical imagination', *Annals, Association of American Geographers* 80 (1990) pp. 418-434; see also Wolfgang Schivelbusch, *The railway journey: the industrialization of time and space in the nineteenth century* (Berkeley CA: University of California Press, 1986) (first published in German 1977) pp. 33-44.

[18] This seems to me the central weakness of Stephen Kern's otherwise suggestive account of *The culture of time and space 1880-1918* (Cambridge, MA: Harvard University Press, 1983): it is a mistake to speak of 'culture' in the singular.

[19] Jürgen Habermas, *The structural transformation of the public sphere* (Cambridge, MA: MIT Press, 1989) (first published in German, 1962). The collection edited by Craig Calhoun, *Habermas and the public sphere* (Cambridge, MA: MIT Press, 1992) is similarly silent about transnational public spheres. For critical discussion, see John Thompson, *The media and modernity* (Cambridge: Polity Press, 1995).

these flows profoundly affected the public consciousness of time. In the closing decades of the century, for example, a newspaper editor in Australia had to fashion a connected narrative of European events by gutting detailed press reports from British newspapers that had reached him by sea, all of them at least three weeks old, and trying to connect them to a tantalisingly brief telegraph message of perhaps 20 code-words that summarised events of the previous 48 hours. It was extraordinarily difficult for editors and readers to reconcile the two, especially when events moved with the rapidity of the Franco-Prussian war of 1870-71 whose speed at once heralded a new phase of modern warfare and captured the imagination of a global audience. In circumstances like these, the compilation of press reports did not reproduce a modernity measured by the intervals of what Benjamin called a 'homogeneous, empty time'; on the contrary, it revealed a manifold of *different* temporalities *shot through with the irruptions of a differential geography*. It was not just that colonial spaces were wired into a grid that was dominated however precariously by metropolitan Europe. These circuits of public information were also underwritten by an imperial *geography of truth*. Thus reports of distant events were seen by a white Australian public as much more coherent and much more reliable if they had been gathered by British news agencies and transmitted through the wires of an 'all-British' cable network.[20] No doubt other colonialisms tell other stories, and by the end of the twentieth century the relations between the global circulation of information, the production of imaginative geographies and the registration of truth claims have become more complicated.[21] But the basic point remains a sharp one: time-space compression produces a striated field of ridges and grooves, asymmetries and inequalities, and mapping its changing geographies discloses many of the most intimate connections between power, the production of space and the constitution of human subjects.

Globalization, localization and the production of place

Secondly, the recovery of these compound geographies of time-space compression calls into question those grand narratives of globalization in which the 'global' progressively erases the 'local'. Our critical histories of space have typically been written as a narrative of triumph and tragedy. According to this scenario, modernity is realized through the projection of an abstract, rational, planned *space* that produces a collective alienation from the concrete particularities of *place*. To be sure, the

---

[20] See my 'Birds on the wire', in *The colonial present* (Oxford UK and Cambridge MA: Blackwell, forthcoming).

[21] See David Morley, Kevin Robins, *Spaces of identity: global media, electronic landscapes and cultural boundaries* (London: Routledge, 1995).

vocabularies differ, and the space of modernity has been variously represented as an optical-geometrical-phallocentric space, a panoptical-partitioned-disciplined space, and a measured-directed-standardized space. The examples could be multiplied many times over, and some of you may detect in the margins of these accounts faint echoes of Habermas's colonization of the lifeworld by the system. Whatever their vocabularies, however, these characterizations of modern space share an insistent *performativity:* they are all versions of what Julie Graham and Kathy Gibson have called a 'rape script'. They describe this narrative as a developing series of steps and signals in which (in the case that concerns them) the global economy of capitalism comes to be represented as both transcendently powerful and inherently spatializing. They object to this as a 'rape script', trading on the shocking imagery of their source-metaphor, because they say it works to normalize an act of non-reciprocal penetration in which all non-capitalist (or non-modern) forms inevitably become damaged, violated, fallen; mastered by the spaces of an advancing modernity, they are sites of a lack, always and everywhere impending targets of invasion, submission, 'colonization'.[22]

I am painting with broad brush-strokes, of course, and I hope you will forgive my simplifications. But in the place of this one-dimensional narrative, a politics of space adequate to the anticipatory-utopian promises of critical theory – or, as I would now prefer, adequate to the project of a radical democracy – needs to develop multi-dimensional narratives that transgress the conventional couplings of triumph and tragedy, possession and innocence, domination and resistance, and which instead disclose complex, foliated spaces of *transculturation*. Mary Louise Pratt describes these spaces as sites of the 'contact zone', spaces of colonial encounter – or what Nicholas Thomas calls 'colonial entanglement' – in which cultures interpenetrate and interrupt one another. Such contact zones have become the exemplary sites of a contemporary 'cosmopolitanism', generalised as the impure condition of (post)modern spatiality, but multidimensionality must not reduce them to equivalence: spaces of transculturation are still tense and unequal, riven by relations of conflict, coercion and co-option.[23]

We also need to discover why these instrumental narratives of globalization have exercised such a fateful hold over so many of us. Perhaps they are all masculinist fantasies? Several feminist critics have suggested that time-space compression

---

[22] J.K. Gibson-Graham, 'Querying globalization', in *The end of capitalism (as we knew it): a feminist critique of political economy* (Oxford UK and Cambridge MA: Blackwell, 1997) pp. 120-147.

[23] Mary Louise Pratt, *Imperial eyes: transculturation and travel writing* (London and New York: Routledge, 1992) pp. 5-7; Nicholas Thomas, *Entangled objects: exchange, material culture and colonialism in the Pacific* (Cambridge MA: Harvard University Press, 1991). For a powerful statement of the exploitations and oppressions implicated in contemporary ideologies of cosmopolitanism, see Timothy Brennan, *At home in the world: cosmopolitanism now* (Cambridge MA: Harvard University Press, 1997) pp. 88-97.

induces such a profound sense of foreboding and disorientation in writers like Harvey because it threatens to dissolve the certainty of their masculinist subject-position and renders its conventional cartographies of power all but useless.[24] If Gibson-Graham's argument is accepted, however, it seems more likely that these rape scripts work to reinscribe – to re-enact – precisely those masculinist powers and privileges. In the face of just this possibility, some feminist geographers have started to rethink traditional conceptions of place, to find ways of treating place as something other than self-enclosing and inward-looking, as something more than a site to be hollowed out and emptied of its supposedly 'essential' or 'local' meaning by the ravages of a transcendent, globalizing capitalism.

This involves not only new ways of thinking theoretically about the very idea of a place; it also requires new forms of fieldwork and new modes of representation. Thus Doreen Massey has urged us to invest in a *politics of place* that is also a *poetics of place*. This is a project that refuses to draw boundaries between the 'inside' and the 'outside' of a place but which treats the production of place as a patchwork of different social threads of varying lengths that are always being woven together in time and space. Massey describes this as a 'global sense of place' that dissolves any idea of place as fixed and frozen. On the contrary, places are always produced, always in process, everywhere implicated in longer social networks. To Massey, this is an inherently progressive sense of place that is directed towards thinking of places as condensations in the contact zone, 'meeting places', hybrid spaces in which identities are conditional products of different encounters.[25]

This is not a difficult idea to understand, at least in outline, but to *convey* this global sense of place requires a revitalization of the powers of geographical description, and in many ways this is much more difficult. Indeed, I suspect that the grand narratives of globalization have become as powerful as they have in some part because too many of us still think of 'description' as somehow simple and straightforward in contradistinction to 'analysis' which is privileged as the more important intellectual task. The sort of theory that informs much of contemporary human geography ought to disqualify the separations between the two, it seems to me, and to restore the hermeneutic circle between them. If we were to take the problematic of

---

[24] See, for example, Rosalyn Deutsche, 'Boys town', reprinted in revised form in her *Evictions: art and spatial politics* (Cambridge, MA: MIT Press, 1997) pp. 203-244; Meaghan Morris, 'The man in the mirror: David Harvey's "Condition" of postmodernity', *Theory, Culture and Society* 9 (1992) pp. 253-79. For his response, see David Harvey, 'Postmodern morality plays', *Antipode* 24 (1992) pp. 300-326.

[25] Doreen Massey, 'Power-geometry and a progressive sense of place', in Jon Bird, Barry Curtis, Tim Putnam, George Robertson and Lisa Tickner (eds.) *Mapping the futures: local cultures, global change* (London: Routledge, 1993) pp. 59-69; Doreen Massey, 'The conceptualization of place', in Doreen Massey and Pat Jess (eds.), *A place in the world: places, cultures and globalization* (Oxford: Oxford University Press, 1995) pp. 45-85.

representation more seriously, to understand that it requires both theoretical reflection and empirical engagement, then perhaps we would be more sensitive to the particularities (and paradoxes) of places and more attentive to the achievements (and ambivalences) of the people that live in them.[26] A critical poetics of place would certainly make it more difficult to think in purely defensive terms about the politics of place.

But other poetics are possible, and it may be that the metanarratives of globalization have assumed such power because they allow the free play of a thoroughly modernist fantasy. They conjure up what Louis Aragon called, much earlier in this century, 'the vertigo of the modern': a world of dizzying speed and increasing abstraction in which the very humanness of our lives is sensibly diminished. Many writers suggest that this process has been radicalized in the closing decades of the twentieth century. According to Manuel Castells, for example, 'space is [increasingly] dissolved into flows', so that many of us now inhabit what he calls 'the space of collective alienation and individual violence' in which 'life is transformed into abstraction, cities into shadows.'[27] This kind of imagery has turned out to be extremely seductive. There is a brooding, menacing quality to much fin-de-siècle theorizing – a theory *noir,* as it were – which mobilizes a masculinist sensibility that aestheticizes and in some cases even delights in the violence of abstraction and the visceral 'hollowing-out' of place.[28]

Some of you will know the influential essay by the American critic Fredric Jameson, in which he uses the Bonaventure Hotel in Los Angeles as a way of conveying the experience of 'hyperspace' that he takes to be symptomatic of the condition of postmodernity. This new spatiality is 'impossible to seize', so he claims: 'bewildering'. Although 'you are in this hyperspace up to your eyes and your body', this architectural 'mutation' has 'succeeded in transcending the capacities of the individual human body to locate itself.' This is Aragon's *Paris Paysan* translated into middle-class America with a vengeance, and Jameson even invokes Benjamin's reading of Baudelaire to secure a figurative disassociation between body-space and

---

[26] Cf. Timothy Oakes, 'Place and the paradox of modernity, *Annals, Association of American Geographers* 87 (1997) pp. 509-531.

[27] Manuel Castells, *The city and the grassroots: a cross-cultural theory of urban social movements* (Berkeley: University of California Press, 1983) p. 314. See also his *The information age: economy, society and culture.* Vol. I: *The rise of the network society* (Oxford UK and Cambridge MA: Blackwell, 1996) and Vol. II: *The power of identity* (Oxford UK and Cambridge MA: Blackwell, 1997). In these later writings, Castells reaffirms his belief in a disjunction between the global and the local and treats the search for meaning and the fabrication of identity as a defensive project, so that the contemporary 'information age' becomes framed by 'unidentified flows and secluded identities.'

[28] Cf. Rosalyn Deutsche, 'Chinatown, Part Four?', in her Evictions *op. cit.*, pp. 245-253.

the space of the city.²⁹ Now Jameson's essay is clever writing, and many middle-aged academics might well become disoriented in such a setting (though in the years since his essay was first published many more of them must have become accustomed to these convention-hotels). But what of the porters, waiters, chefs, maids, and janitors who work in the Bonaventure Hotel? Are we to suppose that they were equally lost in this vast 'hyperspace'? that they were unable to 'map' the building? that they failed to devise their own, highly skilled tactics to cope with the strategies of management and guests? If these possibilities are granted, as I think they must, Jameson's particular experience of the Bonaventure Hotel is scarcely indicative of a general 'postmodern sublime'.

It might be objected that the target is too easy, however, because a building – any building, no matter what its excesses – is too readily mapped as a known 'place'. Indeed, even as he tantalizes his readers with the sheer impossibility of describing this hyperspace, Jameson is also surreptitiously mastering its mobile geometries and categorising their effects. So perhaps we should look elsewhere. For many critics of (post)modernity the spaces of the global regimes of flexible accumulation, disorganised capitalism, casino capitalism – again the terms differ – are much more effective at conveying the limit-experience that Jameson has in mind. In the turbulent world of international finance surely we enter a space of abstraction and alienation? Here, surely, space has been evacuated of all rationality and regulation? Here, finally, space has been annihilated by time? On the contrary. In an important study of the City of London, Nigel Thrift has shown that

> 'The hypermobile world of international money is actually a *hypersocial* world, a world of constant interchange between people, whether over electronic networks, or in face-to-face meetings, or at the end of often lengthy journeys. *In this sense the world of flows is not abstract at all – it is the product of and it is produced by people communicating about what is going on.*'³⁰

In short, the production of everyday life as a skilled accomplishment, a series of richly social practices, is not something which takes place apart from and as a compliant or defiant response to time-space compression: rather, it is *part of* the same bundle of processes and contributes – actively, creatively – to the production of the paradoxical spaces of the modern world.

---

[29] Frederic Jameson, 'The cultural logic of late capitalism', in his *Postmodernism, or the cultural logic of late capitalism* (London: Verso, 1991) pp. 1-54; the first version of this essay was published in 1984.

[30] Nigel Thrift, 'A hyperactive world', in R.J. Johnston, Peter J. Taylor and Michael J. Watts (eds.), *Geographies of global change: remapping the world in the late twentieth century* (Oxford UK and Cambridge MA: Blackwell, 1995) pp. 18-35 (my emphases); see also Nigel Thrift, 'A phantom state? International money, electronic networks and global cities' in his *Spatial formations* (London: Sage, 1996) pp. 213-255 and 'New urban eras and old technological fears: reconfiguring the good will of electronic things', in Andrew Leyshon and Nigel Thrift, *Money/Space: geographies of monetary transformation* (London: Routledge, 1997) pp. 323-54.

Situated knowledges and travelling theories

Thirdly, these successive redescriptions of time-space compression show that theory endows us with the imaginative capacity to reconfigure the world: this is what theory *does*. It follows that a critical history of space has to understand that 'finding things together' is an active process, a political-intellectual practice, in short, *work*. Most of us would I think now accept that this is also, in part, a matter of 'finding ourselves'. Since we do not occupy an Archimedean point from which we can map space as a transparent surface – since we cannot perform what Donna Haraway calls 'the god-trick of seeing everything from nowhere' – we are always both creatures and creators of *situated knowledges*. We must always struggle to grasp our own partiality, so that our understanding of the situatedness of our knowledge is itself partial, incomplete, ambiguous and vulnerable.[31]

My own discipline has made much of this vital insight, so that it has become a commonplace to remark that our theories are marked by their origins. This has cleared the ground for a new history of geography or, more accurately, an historical geography of geography, that recovers what David Livingstone calls 'the spaces of knowledge', the topographies of the multiple sites at which knowledge is produced and the capillary networks through which it is circulated.[32] I very much welcome interventions like these, because the histories we construct enter into the formation of our identities as scholars; if we wish to change our geographies then we must also re-write our historical geographies. But I want to insist that the situatedness of geographical knowledge produces a *double* geography.

On the one side, as Livingstone indicates, this formal geographical imaginary maps a hierarchy of *spaces of knowledge production* in which some sites are valorized as more central than others. Within the dominant intellectual formation of Anglo-American geography, for example, these sites would include the academy (which marginalizes the production of corporate, lay and popular geographies), the universities, journals, societies and meetings that compose Anglo-American geography itself (which marginalizes other geographical discourses), and a rotating grid of other disciplines and intellectual formations (once political economy; then sociology and social theory; now cultural studies and 'French theory'). Other disciplines require other maps, though I would be surprised if they were radically incommensurable with this one; so too do those discourses which advertise their occupation of an interdisciplinary

---

[31] Donna Haraway, 'Situated knowledge: the science question in feminism and the privilege of partial perspective', in her *Simians, cyborgs and women: the reinvention of nature* (London: Routledge, 1991) pp. 183-201; see also Gillian Rose, 'Situating knowledges: positionalities, reflexivities and other tactics', *Progress in Human Geography* 21 (1997) pp. 305-320.

[32] David Livingstone, 'The spaces of knowledge: contributions towards a historical geography of science', *Environment and Planning D: Society & Space* 13 (1995) pp. 5-34.

space, since they do not escape the situatedness of knowledge either. All of our studies are punctuated by and produced through what Bruno Latour calls 'centres of calculation' that 'mobilise, cumulate and recombine the world' through the production of a thoroughly material hierarchy of representational spaces.[33]

On the other side, however, and much less often remarked, this same imaginary sustains a hierarchy of *sites of study* in which some places are valorized as canonical or exotic, as exemplary sites of consuming interest, whereas others are marginalized as merely other, less interesting or less instructive instances of more general conditions that are better exemplified elsewhere. This is partly the product of ethnocentrism, and I should say at once that other disciplines – particularly the humanities – have been much more scrupulous than my own discipline in exploring the constitution of their canon and much less reluctant to learn from other traditions.[34] Unfortunately modern (and postmodern) geography, like charity, seems to begin at home and all too often to remain there. These limitations are given a special inflection by a series of theoretical closures. It's not difficult to deconstruct the mappings of Ango-American spatial science: the circumscribed world of isotropic planes in which Iowa was constituted as the epitome of all marketing systems – how rapidly Southern Germany was eclipsed! – and Chicago as the model for all modern cities. Yet the same sort of moves underwrite more recent and self-consciously critical claims that treat Los Angeles as 'the' postmodern city – 'a paradigmatic place', 'the epitomizing world-city'[35] – or India as the canonical instance of colonial history in general (in its way, a remarkably colonial manoeuvre) and hence the privileged site for the production of an oppositional postcolonialism.[36]

Sites of knowledge production and sites of study are thus hooked up within what Gillian Rose identifies as a 'specular spatiality': a territory 'into which some are gathered and from which others are exiled.'[37] This double geography of power-knowledge means that time-space compression is inscribed within the very conduct

---

[33] Ibid; Bruno Latour, *Science in action* (Cambridge MA: Harvard University Press, 1987). See also Joseph Rouse, *Knowledge and power: toward a political philosophy of science* (Ithaca: Cornell University Press, 1987).

[34] Cf. David Slater, 'On the borders of social theory: learning from other regions', *Environment and Planning D: Society & Space* 10 (1992) pp. 307-327.

[35] Soja, Postmodern geographies *op. cit.*, p. 221.

[36] This is not to vitiate the achievements of the scholars associated with *Subaltern Studies*, nor to minimise the interest of the debates that surround their work. But it is to emphasise the *specificity* of their project and its political-intellectual address.

[37] Gillian Rose, 'Tradition and paternity: same difference?' *Transactions, Institute of British Geographers* 20 (1995) pp. 414-416. Rose's argument is another version of Foucault's distinction between 'the history of the Other' – the history of that which a cultural formation excludes and closes off – and 'the history of the Same' – 'the history of the order imposed on things ... and collected together into identities': see Michel Foucault, *The order of things* (London: Tavistock, 1970) p. xxiv.

of our studies, and that it contracts our imaginative and interpretive geographies in ways that we are only now beginning to uncover. Yet this does not condemn us to a debilitating parochialism. As I read Haraway's essay on situated knowledges, its key message is that theory does more than delimit our worlds: it also makes it possible to 'de-limit' our worlds. There is, of course, a real danger that theory in this expansive sense – what Edward Said once called 'travelling theory' – all too readily converts into an imperial gesture of aggrandisement and appropriation. There are many instances of theory, freed from its empirical particulars, roaming free as a mobile form of cultural capital to be reinvested in the double geography I have just described.[38] But Haraway invites each of us to reach out from our particular positions in order to construct webs of connection, lines of flight *whose arguments do not deny difference but which also recognize mutuality*. The construction of these webs of connection – circuits of conversation and circles of solidarity – enters into the very object-ness of our world, Haraway argues, and requires us to attend with all possible care to a process of 'putting things together' which she calls *articulation*. She trades on both meanings of that term, so that her critical practice involves both mobilising connections between separate 'partners' and releasing their different 'voices'. 'Articulation is always a non-innocent, contestable practice,' she warns, and its outcome is always uncertain: more prosaically, 'articulation© is work and it may fail.' As Haraway describes her project, it involves confounding our taken-for-granted distinctions and recognising the hybrid, co-constructedness of our world.[39] In much the same spirit, I suggest that a critical history of 'finding things together' requires us to contaminate the purity of our metanarratives of time-space compression and recover the historically and geographically determinate ways in which 'space' and 'place' have been articulated.

Although Haraway's recent writings provide insights into the powers that inhere in productions of space and place, she is much more interested in muddying the historically sedimented separations between 'culture' and 'nature'.[40] The two problematics are closely connected, however, and so I want to turn to the

---

[38] Edward Said, 'Travelling theory', in his *The world, the text and the critic* (London: Faber and Faber, 1984) pp. 226-47; for a commentary on European high theory as symbolic capital, see Vivek Dhareshwar, 'The predicament of theory', in Martin Kreiswirth and Mark Cheetham (eds.) *Theory between the disciplines: authority/vision/politics* (Ann Arbor: University of Michigan Press, 1990) pp. 230-50. Footloose theory has been underwritten by the globalization of academic publishing and the restructuring of many universities as transnational corporations: see Bill Readings, *The university in ruins* (Cambridge MA: Harvard University Press, 1997).

[39] Haraway, 'Situated knowledges' *op. cit*; see also Trevor Barnes and Derek Gregory, 'Worlding geography: geography as situated knowledge', in *Reading human geography: the poetics and politics of inquiry* (London: Arnold, 1997) pp. 14-26.

[40] Donna Haraway, *Modest_Witness@Second Millenium. FemaleMan© _Meets_OncoMouse™: Feminism and Technoscience* (New York: Routledge, 1997).

implications for my own argument of an observation made many years ago by the philosopher A.N. Whitehead: 'Nature doesn't come as clean as you can think it.'

Questions of nature

Let me return to Hegel, whose *Lectures on the philosophy of world history*, first delivered in 1822-23, depended on a concept of nature. There are many figures who stand behind Hegel, writers whose ideas cast long shadows across his desk, but I want to pay particular attention to Karl Ritter and his comparative geography. 'There can be no speculation,' Ritter declared, 'no philosophy of the unlimited and eternal, without inquiry into and knowledge of the limited and conditional.' It was a task of the first importance, so he believed, to 'learn the limits of the realm which Man makes his home and to understand all its secrets ... so as to turn them to his own uses.'[41] In much the same way, in part through his association with Ritter at the University of Berlin, Hegel saw 'nature' as a foundation – his exact words were a 'geographical basis' – for his philosophy of history.

> 'Man uses nature for his own ends; but where nature is too powerful it does not allow itself to be used as a means.... The torrid and frigid zones, as such, are not the theatre on which world history is enacted.... All in all, it is therefore the temperate zone which must furnish the theatre of history. And more specifically the northern part of the temperate zone....'[42]

These were not exceptional views in nineteenth-century Europe, and I want to identify two discursive strategies that are mobilised in accounts like them.

Discrimination, domination and the dialectic of Enlightenment

The first strategy involves what I will call the discrimination of nature. According to this view, pre-modern or non-modern cultures are at one with nature, intimately embedded in and even indistinguishable from their surrounding ecologies, whereas modern cultures are *distinguished* by their *distance* from and *domination* over nature.

Claims like these were given special force in early modern Europe, when 'disordered, active nature' was forced to submit to the probes of a new, experimental science, and when marshes and fenlands were reclaimed by the pumps of a new, mechanical technology. Indeed, it has been argued that it was the intimate conjunction between science and technology in the sixteenth and seventeenth centuries that licensed a new sense of human domination over nature. This sensibility was codified

---

[41] Karl Ritter, *Comparative geography* (trans. William Gage) (Philadelphia: Lippincott, 1865).
[42] G.W.F. Hegel, *Lectures on the philosophy of history* (Cambridge: Cambridge University Press, 1975 edn.) p. 155.

in a profoundly gendered and sexualized imaginary. Henceforth 'the constraints against penetration associated with the earth-mother image [of Renaissance "nature"] were transformed into sanctions for denudation,' Carolyn Merchant writes, so that a feminized *Natura* could no longer complain 'that her garments of modesty [were] being torn by the wrongful thrusts of man.'[43] This evidently enacts another 'rape-script', and it is one that had a powerful presence in the projects of European colonialism. While Merchant's argument unfolds in a Europe riven by the scientific revolution of the sixteenth and seventeenth centuries, there were intricate connections between the maps of nature made by that 'new science' and the mappings of the 'New World'.[44]

The discourse of discrimination achieved still greater prominence in the eighteenth century. In 1778, the comte de Buffon, superintendent of the Jardin du Roi in Paris, identified the last of his seven *époques de la nature* as an age in which human beings became something more than frightened animals in a terrible and terrifying nature. They set about transforming nature, Buffon argued, to such effect that 'with the help of our hands' – through human intervention and artifice – Nature had progressively arrived at what he took to be its present 'point of perfection.' While Buffon recognized the previous achievements of other cultures, especially in Asia, it was the modern European domestication of nature that occupied the central, crowning place in his history. 'Wild nature is hideous and dying,' he wrote; 'it is I, I alone, who can make it agreeable and living.'[45]

The domestication of Buffon's 'wild nature' was thus caught up in discourses of 'civilization', of 'progress', of what we would now identify as capitalist modernity, and it is scarcely surprising that contemporary critical theory and political ecology should have seen close connections between the human domination of nature and the instrumentalities of the European Enlightenment. We have become quite properly cautious about speaking of 'the' Enlightenment, however, and the same reservations should be attached to the ideologies of nature that were developed under its sign. To recognize the complexity of Alexander von Humboldt's constructions of

---

[43] Carolyn Merchant, *The death of nature: women, ecology and the scientific revolution* (New York: Harper and Row, 1980) pp. 164, 189.

[44] See Denise Albanese, 'Admiring Miranda and enslaving Nature', in her *New science, New World* (Durham: Duke University Press, 1996) pp. 59-91. There were equally vital connections between the new science, the New World and the formation of a recognisably 'modern' geography: see David Livingstone, 'Revolution, celestial and terrestrial: Geography and the scientific revolution', in his *The geographical tradition: episodes in the history of a contested enterprise* (Oxford UK and Cambridge MA: Blackwell, 1992) pp. 63-101.

[45] Clarence Glacken, *Traces on the Rhodian shore* (Berkeley: University of California Press, 1967) pp. 496, 663-8. Glacken's study was intended to be the first volume of a larger history but unfortunately he never lived to bring the second volume to print. For my purposes, *Traces* comes to an end just as the story starts to become really interesting.

nature, for example, and their imbrication in both a lyrical romanticism and the project of a global physics, is to concede that the articulation of human domination of nature was far from unequivocal.[46] While I think it is an exaggeration to propose a distinctively 'green imperialism', as Richard Grove has sought to do, it is none the less necessary to recognise the diversity of cultures (including cultures of natural history and natural science) through which 'nature' was constructed within a European grid of concepts that made it available to political and economic calculation.[47]

The singular emphasis on calculation – on the realization of what Habermas would have once called a technical interest – is significant, even so, because it formed the mainspring of the 'dialectic of Enlightenment'. Although the basic argument was intimated by Max Horkheimer and Theodor Adorno, it was developed most forcefully by Herbert Marcuse. Even as modern science 'mastered' nature, holding out the prospect of a humankind freed from the privations of hunger and the ravages of disease, so Marcuse argued that it was casting the bars of Weber's 'iron cage': 'The ever-more-effective domination of nature thus came to provide the pure concepts as well as the instrumentalities for the ever-more-effective domination of man by man *through* the domination of nature.'[48]

These arguments can be extended in various ways. Given their provenance, it is only to be expected that they would accord a central place to domination through a nexus of class relations; but they fail to consider the implications of the gendering of their constructions. This is a central issue for ecofeminism, of course, and it is intertwined with two others. Neither the concepts nor the instrumentalities that Marcuse identified were confined to nominally scientific discourse, which was the principal object of his critique, and the feminisation of nature can be seen in many other cultural registers. Indeed, it was the tensile connections between different (phallocentric) discourses that allowed the domination of nature to seem so 'natural'.

---

[46] See Michael Dettelbach, 'Global physics and aesthetic empire: Humboldt's physical portrait of the tropics', in David Miller and Hans Peter Reill (eds.), *Visions of empire: voyages, botany and representations of nature* (Cambridge: Cambridge University Press, 1996) pp. 258-292.

[47] Richard Grove, *Green imperialism: colonial expansion, tropical island Edens and the origins of environmentalism 1600-1800* (Cambridge: Cambridge University Press, 1995); cf. N. Jardine, J.A. Secord and E.C. Spary (eds.) *Cultures of natural history* (Cambridge: Cambridge University Press, 1996).

[48] Max Horkheimer and Theodor Adorno, *Dialectic of Enlightenment* (New York: Continuum, 1990) (first published in German, 1944); Herbert Marcuse, *One-dimensional man* (London: Abacus, 1972) p. 130. The continuities with Habermas and later writers are explored in Robyn Eckersley, 'Habermas and green political thought', *Theory and Society* 19 (1990) pp. 739-76; Matthew Gandy, 'Ecology, modernity and the legacy of the Frankfurt School', in Andrew Light and Jonathan Smith (eds.) *Space, place and environmental ethics*, being *Philosophy and Geography* 12 (1997) pp. 231-254. See also David Harvey, 'The domination of nature and its discontents', in his *Justice, nature and the geography of difference* (Oxford UK and Cambridge MA: Blackwell, 1996) pp. 120-149.

Neither were those concepts and instrumentalities limited to the production and penetration of a purely 'Western' nature: Marcuse said little enough about it, but the domination of other natures was of strategic importance to the colonisation of other cultures. These twin cautions prompt large questions, but I raise them here only to propose that the domination of other natures – their colonisation by a globalizing Reason spinning around its aesthetic, scientific and moral axes – was always an ambivalent gesture. To European writers, other natures could be sites of savagery – like the formless, un-nameable 'horror' of the African rainforest in Joseph Conrad's *Heart of Darkness* – or they could be intimations of paradise: which is how many European explorers saw the islands of the South Pacific at the close of the eighteenth century.[49] And as I now want to show, this ambivalence was not a nervous tic at the extremities of empire; it was, rather, a vital, constitutive dynamic within the geographical imaginary of post-Enlightenment Europe, where it was managed and contained through a second discursive strategy.

The normalization of nature

This second strategy involves what I want to call the normalization of nature. When Foucault mapped the emergence of *disciplinary power* as a characteristically modern form of power, he developed an analytics of *space* to show how 'docile bodies' were assigned their 'proper places': how the normalization of the human subject depended upon the production of a panoptical-partitioned-disciplinary space. And yet in what I take to be his parallel argumentation-sketch of the formation of *bio-power*, which he described as 'the entry of life into history' by means of which 'Western man was gradually learning what it meant to be a living species in a living world', Foucault was strangely silent about the analytics of *nature* and its implication in the normalization of the human subject.[50]

---

[49] David Arnold, 'Inventing tropicality', in his *The problem of nature: environment, culture and European expansion* (Oxford UK and Cambridge MA: Blackwell, 1996) pp. 141-168.

[50] Michel Foucault, *Discipline and punish: the birth of the prison* (London: Penguin, 1977) (first published in French, 1975); Michel Foucault, *The history of sexuality: an introduction* (London: Penguin, 1981) (first published in French, 1976) pp. 135-145. These two texts stand in the closest of associations – Foucault started work on the second as soon as he had completed the first – but there is a shift of emphasis between them. *Discipline and punish* is concerned with the 'normalization of power', whereas *The history of sexuality* is concerned with the 'power of normalization': see Ann Laura Stoler, *Race and the education of desire: Foucault's "History of sexuality" and the colonial order of things* (Durham: Duke University Press, 1995). Neil Smith has long since argued for a close connection between the production of space and the production of nature, but he identified these twin thematics with the production of class-subjects alone: see his *Uneven development : nature, capital and the production of space* (Oxford UK and Cambridge MA: Blackwell, 1990; this was first published in 1984).

63

I can best indicate what I have in mind by returning to Ritter's comparative geography. 'The constitution of the globe is incontestably coincident with a plan to preserve and perfect Man,' he argued. 'There are destructive agencies, it is true, but they do not operate on an extended scale; earthquakes and volcanoes, and great storms at sea, affect but a portion of the race, they are no longer universal in their action.'[51] I don't think it difficult to identify which 'Man' Ritter took to be the terminus of this project of perfection. It was bourgeois man (and the class and gender ascriptions are significant); and it was also unquestionably European man, Foucault's 'Western man', who was – *by his very nature* – 'temperate' man. This is not the place to describe the genealogy of this ideology of nature in any detail, but temperate nature was produced and reproduced across a vast array of European discursive fields – textualized, visualized and classified in travel-writing, in art, in natural history – as *normal* nature. As such it implied the repudiation of extremes and the achievement of environmental stability. As Ritter insisted, the 'destructive agencies' that he enumerated were 'no longer universal in their action'. The violence of an intemperate nature, red in tooth and claw, was distant from Europe in geological time or geographical space: ice ages, earthquakes and volcanoes, tempests and typhoons were not the dominant motifs of temperate nature. I remember an old Bill Tidy cartoon in which a Victorian policeman strolled along a beach with a megaphone instructing British holiday-makers to 'Roll up your trousers! Krakatoa has exploded!' Disasters on the other side of the world attracted attention, even excitement, and there were occasional cataclysms much closer to home. But for the most part environmental ruptures were the exception that proved the temperate rule. Equally dissonant from the harmony of temperate nature was the siren song of a seductive, sultry and feminised tropical nature. The European colonisation of the tropics cast environmental determinism in a new and even menacing light – would these regions become 'the white man's grave'? – but if there was a 'moral economy of climate', as Livingstone suggests, it was one that consistently emphasised the virtues and, by implication, the normalization of temperate regimes.[52]

The strategy of normalization presented at once an opportunity and a dilemma. On the one side, it made it possible for European writers to talk about 'culture' by talking about 'nature' in a different register. Other cultures were not only represented as creatures of other natures – captives of Nature's caprice – but they were also seen as in some sense *deviant* creatures of *deviant* natures. When the young Florence Nightingale visited Egypt in the winter of 1849-50, for example, she wanted to claim the monumental achievements of ancient Egypt – its temples and tombs –

---

[51] Ritter, Comparative geography *op. cit.*
[52] David Livingstone, 'The moral discourse of climate: historical considerations on race, place and virtue', *Journal of Historical Geography* 17 (1991) pp. 413-34.

as the cradle of a distinctively European civilisation. In order to do so, she distanced that ancient world from the cultures of nineteenth-century Egypt by reducing the contemporary inhabitants of Egypt to the brutal denizens of what she repeatedly described as 'an unnatural Nature'. On the other side, however, it was necessary to find the terms for – to come to terms with – this 'unnatural', deviant and diabolical nature. Nightingale fretted that it was 'useless to try to describe these things, for European language has no words for them.'

> 'How should it, when there is no such thing in Europe? All other nature raises one's thoughts to heaven: this sends them to hell.'[53]

Here, then, was the rub: could these strange – uncanny, *unheimlich* – landscapes be brought within a European project of earth-writing, of literally 'geo-graphing', conducted under the sign of a sovereign Reason? Paul Carter's vivid account of *The road to Botany Bay* describes the bewilderment of the early European explorers and surveyors travelling through the Australian interior. They had to find a way of making the land submit to the demand that the English language offer what Carter calls 'a more coherent rhetorical equivalent, a more logical arrangement of what was to be seen' than any native language. They were armed with an arsenal of European devices for ordering the world – taxonomic grids, co-ordinate geometries, linear perspectives, picturesque views – which entered into the formation of what Pratt sees as a new and distinctively European planetary consciousness, a system of global unity and order devised and directed by the metropolitan cultures at the heart of empire.[54] But as Pratt shows, this was never a simple and self-confident process. Underwriting the project 'of reducing the world to uniformity, replacing local difference with universal intelligibility', as Carter describes it, was something approaching panic. Thus European explorers were horrified to find that the interior of Australia was not occupied by what, in a splendid phrase, Carter calls 'purposeful rivers':

> 'Quite the contrary, rather than myriad trickles combining and contributing to form major rivers, the tendency was for flood water to spread out, to disperse through a lacework of temporary channels which, far from concentrating the water, fanned it out to cover huge areas of normally waterless desert. Instead of contributing to rivers, watercourses acted as dis-tributaries. *There was nothing intrinsically irrational about this system .... but in the context of the*

---

[53] Florence Nightingale, *Letters from Egypt: a journey on the Nile 1849-1850* (ed. Anthony Sattin) (New York: Weidenfeld and Nicolson,1987) p. 87; for a discussion, see Derek Gregory, 'Between the mirror and the lamp: imaginative geographies of Egypt, 1849-1850', *Transactions, Institute of British Geographers* 20 (1995) pp. 29-57.

[54] Pratt, Imperial eyes *op. cit.*, pp. 29-33. See also Bernard Smith, *European vision and the South Pacific* (New Haven: Yale University Press, 1985) and, more generally, Miller and Reill, Visions of empire *op. cit.*, and Jardine, Secord and Spary, Cultures of natural history *op. cit.*

explorer's responsibility to invest the space of his journey with meaning, they were, politically and economically, unthinkable.[55]

These were more than the field-responses of adventurers and amateurs. Nominally scientific prose made similar normalizing gestures as Nature was colonised by Reason. When the American geographer W.M. Davis proposed his 'ideal' or 'normal' cycle of erosion at the very end of the nineteenth century, to take a particularly egregious example, it was modelled on fluvial temperate regimes. Moving towards the poles or the tropics, he identified 'significant departures from normal geographical development' and these 'accidents', as he termed them, prompted him to propose 'special' cycles of erosion to accommodate them.[56] Davis's ideas achieved extraordinary prominence in Britain, the USA and France, but they were criticised by German-speaking geographers who urged a greater sensitivity to climatic variation in time and space. I am thinking of Siegfried Passarge, Albrecht and Walther Penck, and – most of all – Alfred Hettner, who (significantly) objected to what he called Davis's 'purely geometrical approach' because it produced a landscape of 'moribund and dismal emptiness' incapable of rendering the richness, complexity and variety of the earth's surface.[57]

I hope I have said enough to convey something of the power of the normalization of nature.[58] To be sure, the assumption of a 'normal' nature, a Nature subjected to Reason, is presently being undermined. I am not the person to describe any of this in any detail (perhaps even at all), but there can be no doubt that those of us who live in the West are now experiencing the ravages of an 'unnatural Nature' – raw, volatile, unpredictable – *at home*: dying forests and wetlands, polluted skies and oceans, flooding rivers, soaring temperatures. If 'panic ecologies' are multiplying in our 'risk society', however, these can in part be read as displacements of and interruptions to the ways in which we have normalized a particular conception of nature.[59] And in

---

[55] Paul Carter, *The road to Botany Bay: an essay in spatial history* (London: Faber, 1987) pp. 55-6 (my emphasis). Simon Ryan describes this response as the product of 'the myth of antipodality' in which 'Australia' was figured within the European geographical imaginary as 'a place of perversity, where the norms and nature of Europe are inverted': *The cartographic eye: how explorers saw Australia* (Cambridge: Cambridge University Press, 1996) p. 105.

[56] W.M. Davis, 'The geographical cycle', *Geog. Jnl.* XIV (1899) pp. 481-504; idem, 'Complications of the geographical cycle', *Report of the Eighth International Geographical Congress*, Washington (1904), pp. 150-163; both reprinted in W.M. Davis, *Geographical essays* (Boston: Ginn, 1909).

[57] R.J. Chorley, R.P. Beckinsale, A.J. Dunn, *The history of the study of landforms, or the development of geomorphology*. Vol. 2: *The life and work of William Morris Davis* (London: Methuen, 1973) p. 511.

[58] See also Bruce Willems-Braun, 'Buried epistemologies: the politics of nature in (post)colonial British Columbia', *Annals, Association of American Geographers* 87 (1997) pp. 3-31, especially n. 14.

[59] Cf. Ulrich Beck, *Risk society: towards a new modernity* (London: Sage, 1992); Nigel Clark, 'Panic ecology: Nature in the age of superconductivity', *Theory, Culture and Society* 14 (1997) pp. 77-96.

calling this regime of truth into question, we return once again to the process of articulation: of resisting the conventional separations between 'culture' and 'nature'.

The geographical discourse of modernity

I have tried to argue that there are at least two vital senses in which 'geography' provides a discursive foundation for 'modernity'. I have also suggested that those foundational constructs of 'space' and 'nature' have been rudely disturbed, and that reconstructing the history of these sly spatialities and normalized natures – even in the skeletal forms I have adduced here – ought to make us suspicious of the architecture they once supported. As the modern constellation between rationality, spatiality and nature comes under increasing pressure, in theory and in practice, so we might at last come to question the very concept of modernity itself. Latour has suggested that 'modernity' is a story the West tells itself, setting apart its supposedly rational and universal knowledges from the local and particular knowledges of others; that in repeating its grand narratives we effectively sanctify the West under the sign of a singular, global modernity. In Latour's view, many of the process that I have been describing today hinge on the construction of networks – on that process of articulation to which I have repeatedly referred – so that the more extensive the networks, the more likely the knowledges and practices which they put in place are to be sanctioned as 'true'; others become 'local', 'traditional', outside the space of Reason, confined to and indicative of an 'unnatural Nature'.[60] If this is a persuasive argument, then we need to think instead about spaces of co-existence and connection: hybrid spaces of power, paradox and possibility. For only then, I suggest, will we have arrived at a truly geographical discourse of modernity.

---

[60] Bruno Latour, *We have never been modern* (Cambridge, MA: Harvard University Press, 1993) (first published in French, 1991).

DISCUSSING
IMAGINATIVE GEOGRAPHIES

Discussing imaginative geographies: Derek Gregory on representation, modernity and space [*]

edited by MICHAEL HOYLER

Geographical representations[1]

Over the last years there seems to have emerged a prominent discourse in Anglo-American geographical inquiry that emphasises not so much the analysis of material culture, but the need for a greater sensitivity towards the power of geographical representations in literature, art, politics. How have these questions gained their disciplinary importance and where do you see the specific value of this approach? Could you perhaps illustrate some ways in which such representations are constructed and used?

Derek Gregory: One obvious example with which most of you will be familiar, is the work that was done in the United States and elsewhere in the 1960s and 1970s on mental maps. For ten years or more a great deal of research went into the construction of mental maps and much of this research was very sophisticated indeed. Particular groups in the population were identified and asked to draw mental maps of

---

[*] This documentation presents some of Derek Gregory's spontaneous responses in the lively discussions during four seminars with graduate students accompanying the first Hettner-Lecture at the University of Heidelberg in June 1997. The excerpts printed here touch on many of the current Anglo-American debates that differ substantially from prominent geographical discourses within German-speaking academia. Expressed here in an easily accessible style, Derek Gregory's inspiring ideas might be read as a stimulus for renewed reflection on our own geographical imaginations.
The seminars were moderated by Tim Freytag and Michael Hoyler. Throughout, Henning Banthien and Burkhard Remppis assisted the memory of all participants by making their voices visible on the library walls of the *Villa Bosch*. Special thanks are due to Katharine Reynolds, who committed herself to the difficult task of transcribing speech from hissing tapes, converting transient phonic into space-bound graphic substance. The edited text follows the transcript. I have, however, rephrased the questions put to Derek Gregory and reproduced all seminar discussions in a condensed and less dialogic style.
Readers who would like to delve into the issues discussed will find topical starting points in Trevor Barnes and Derek Gregory (eds.) *Reading human geography: the poetics and politics of inquiry* (London: Arnold, 1997). See also two other recent anthologies: Stephen Daniels and Roger Lee (eds.) *Exploring human geography: a reader* (London: Arnold, 1996), John Agnew, David N. Livingstone and Alisdair Rogers (eds.) *Human geography: an essential anthology* (Oxford, UK and Cambridge, MA: Blackwell, 1996).

[1] *Villa Bosch*, Tuesday, 24th June 1997, 14.30 to 18.00. The discussion started with an exercise in iconographic interpretation – analysing representations of Heidelberg on picture postcards (Renaissance order, Romantic landscape, contemporary tourist gaze, mental map).

their cities, so there were those famous illustrations of middle class groups in Los Angeles – what would they draw on their mental maps? And then the homeless and the down-and-out in Los Angeles, what would they put on their mental maps? This went on for ten years or more, until somebody asked whether people ever *used* mental maps. It was then discovered that the reason people drew mental maps was that they were *asked* to do so by researchers. They were given a piece of paper and a pen and asked, could you just draw a map of ...? But it turns out that most of us, when we find our way around a city, do not start out with a kind of mental atlas and turn over the pages in our heads and there is the plan of Stuttgart or Munich or Heidelberg, and move our way around it. In practice, the way in which we move through cities is much more tactical: we haven't planned a detailed route in advance, but we go along the street and when we see the church it's like a cue in a stage play and at that point we turn right. And we very rarely recover the city as a coherent totality, as a mental map, that's not how we *use* our representations. So it seems to me that the question of how these representations come to be, why some are validated and reproduced again and again and again is not separate from the uses to which they are put. It's not easy to conduct that kind of analysis, I think, for a number of reasons. In very many cases we do what we think we *ought* to do, so we are following a series of norms and conventions, which in a sense validate the experience and validate the knowledge, but which are themselves rarely examined: by convention, our conventions are left alone, unremarked and unanalysed.

This morning walking back from reception in the old Aula to my hotel, I encountered a large party of Japanese tourists walking towards me. What was astonishing was that nobody was looking where they were going. But they all held camcorders, video cameras, and they were walking through the streets of Heidelberg looking at it through a viewfinder [...]. Another example: if you visit the University of Oxford, they market something called the 'Oxford Experience'. Tourists come to Oxford and presumably Heidelberg, and want to know, where is the university? Well, in Oxford that's an impossible question to answer, it's a kind of virtual reality, it doesn't exist as a single entity: there are individual colleges but the university is a concept rather than a site. So the 'Oxford Experience' *constructs* a site, and you can go there and explore through the exhibition Oxford's past and present, and see plans and paintings and photographs. I have been in Oxford and I have watched buses stop, tourists get out, go into this exhibition, spend an hour or so there, get back on the bus and drive on to Bath [...]. The knowledge that people have of Oxford in an experience like this is, again, almost entirely visual. But it is a very particular, focused and directed experience. Framing the world in ways like these has become acceptable, even commonplace at the end of the 20th century; it doesn't seem strange to go to a place and not actually see it, because you can go into an exhibition and see it. In some respects these sights through a viewfinder or staged at an exhibition might even seem more 'authentic' than the places being represented – 'authenticity' is then an effect produced by the *organisation* of the view, its claims to completeness, transparency and even legitimacy.

Representation, then, is always a struggle – a conditional achievement – and those conditions (and consequences) mean that representation is always implicated in the play of *power*. Within our discipline, I think that we've spent rather too much time over the last 20 years worrying about analysis – which *is* difficult and important – and forgetting just how difficult and just how important representation is. To be sure, you cannot separate them very easily – theories are, after all, a way of imaginatively re-presenting the world, exhibiting it in a different light – but I think that we have invested a great deal of effort into the formal construction of theories and models and techniques, and we haven't invested enough time in what seems to me to be so cripplingly difficult: description. When I taught first-year students at Cambridge, they found writing their first essay comparatively simple, because it was an exercise in analysis, and they were used to that and knew what conventions to follow. They found writing their first letter home, describing that strange city and what was happening to them, much more difficult. Description seems to me to be an essential part of what we ought to be doing, and if geography is to remain intellectually alive as a discipline and not to go the way of many of the other social sciences in the English-speaking world, it has to recover that ability to describe places, not according to some formula, some sort of master techniques that we can all learn – I think of those dreadful regional monographs all of which were organised in the same way, in the same sequence, with the same chapter headings – if that was a sensible way of knowing the world then all novels would be written the same way, in the same sequence. It's important politically, it's important morally, it's important intellectually and it's important just to make sure that what we do is *interesting* – to engage the attentions and the emotions of our audience – to be able to describe the places, the people, the landscapes that we are talking about and to have those descriptions called to account. And that means we really do need to think about questions of representation and how they are constructed in writing, in images, in music and elsewhere.

This sort of a discussion is at last under way, but I suspect that many of us are much more comfortable about treating representation as a purely technical matter. So we talk about map reading as a technical exercise – which way is north, how to read the contour lines, how to give a grid reference. But it's much harder to talk about map reading as a *cultural* exercise: why are these things on the map and not these? What assumptions are smuggled onto maps under the sign of a disinterested 'Science'? We use photographs very often as decorations in books, but we don't talk about their composition as *images* very often, presumably because we think you have to be an art historian or a historian of photography to do that. And what about music? As a university professor you spend your days surrounded by young people, who spend their days surrounded by music, and yet the strange thing is how very rarely you talk about it. And yet music, particularly at the end of the 20th century, is a very powerful way of representing places. I mean there are geographies written into music. All of this is just a way of saying that I think the question of representation is not trivial, it's not atheoretical, it's not unimportant, it's actually fundamental.

Geographers often regard analysis as much more important than description. Describing places evokes associations of traditional regional geography lacking theoretical and methodological rigour.

Derek Gregory: Theory enters into the process of description because it's a re-description in a way, so analysis very often can be just another way of describing. But I think that to convey in a lecture, in a book, in an article, to people who have never been to a place something of what that place means to you and to those who live there, your experience of it or other people's experience of it, seems to me to be so important and so difficult.

Paradoxically, description *appears* much easier at the end of the 20th century than it did in the centuries before. At the end of the 18th century, for example, the French invaded Egypt and Napoleon took with him 150 scholars, artists and engineers, who mapped, measured and drew everything in sight. When they returned to France they produced a multi-volume work called 'The description of Egypt'.[2] Its plates were the first detailed – and so seemingly 'realistic' – representations of Egypt presented to a European audience. These were not conventional representations – pure fantasies and imaginary scenes – but they were drawn by people who had been there. Other obvious examples include the sketches and engravings that were produced by the artists and draughtsmen who accompanied Cook on his voyages in the South Pacific, or the accounts published by von Humboldt on his return from South America. All these representations were brought back to a Europe which was set alight by them, which awakened a new sense of *wonder*, and I think in some ways too even a sense of *responsibility* – we might not like the forms that responsibility took, but at least it was a sense of moral *connection*. Now fast forward: at the end of the 20th century it is so easy to sit down and turn on the TV news, and have images stream in – selectively, to be sure – from all over the world. That sense of ease, of facility, of *familiarity*, has dulled that sense of wonder, it's removed that sense of moral connection. So one of the reasons that description and representation have become such a responsibility to us as intellectuals is that most people take them for granted. They are accustomed to having the world displayed before them, they see the world in structured, stereotypical ways. Our task, I think, is to unsettle these conventions, to recover and

---

[2] *Description de l'Egypte ou Recueil des observations et des recherches qui ont été faites en Egypte pendant l'expédition de l'armée française* (Paris: Impr. impériale: puis Impr. royale, 1809-1822).

describe the world in much more interesting ways, in many more multidimensional ways [...]. I think that one of the biggest responsibilities we have as geographers is shaking our students out of that complacent view that they know all this, that they know the world, that it contains no surprises for them, no wonder, and description is really not very difficult [...]. The first job of geography is to make people lost, in a way, to disconcert them, to make them realise that they don't know the world they live in, they really don't, and that it's incredibly *difficult* to know: and then we can talk.

We have learnt to think in dichotomies such as description on the one hand and specialised analysis on the other. The first is considered to be atheoretical, and this view has eventually led to the demise of regional geography. Are geographers today capable of providing the kind of theoretically informed description of places that you have in mind?

Derek Gregory: In the English-speaking world over the last five or ten years there has been much more interest in representation, but for the most part it's been in the *analysis* of representation – in *reading* representations – so that there are very many quite brilliant cultural geographers working in Britain and North America who could tell you far more about these postcards [of Heidelberg] than I could, for example, who know about art history, about the cultural construction of perspective and what happens when you construct the landscape in these particular ways. Equally, of course, there are analyses building on the wonderfully suggestive work of Brian Harley, of the map as an instrument of power, which raises exactly those questions about why is this on the map and not that, is this the view of a white colonising population, and how did native people map their world?

If we have become very good at the analysis of representation and much more critical of it than we were in the past, I don't think that we've got any better at representation itself: we can explain why it's so difficult, why it's important – which is what I've been doing – but what we *do* in producing our own geographies is still very weak in terms of working with representations.

I think too that descriptions are always theoretical. I would say that the most important change in my work in the last five years or so has been a wonderful sense of freedom that comes from realising that no one theory is going to give you everything. There is no single point of view from which everything makes perfect sense. To discover that you did not have to choose between or even agree with Habermas or Giddens, but you could read their work in more critical ways, in ways that they didn't want you to read it, that you could take something from it, but not everything, that you could read 'theory' as a source of ideas but not treat it as a complete, closed and transparent vision of the world – all of this was wonderful. There is a real sense of liberation in realising that, the sociologist Michael Mann says it very well, 'society is much messier than our theories of it', and most of our theories do clean up the world, tidy it up and make it wonderfully ordered so that everything fits together. For years I lived in two worlds, one a 'theoretical' universe where intellectually and theoretically everything balanced, and the other much more mundane, ordinary and grubby, where things never seemed to quite come together.

But thinking and working in the spaces *between* different theoretical systems is also uncomfortable, not least because it means you can never stop reading, you can't say, well I've surveyed the field and I've decided that (say) Habermas or Giddens has said the last word. You can't stop reading and, in consequence, you can't hide the contradictions. These people don't all say the same thing, and you can't round off the edges and fit them all together, and assume that if you take a bit of Foucault, a bit of Habermas and a bit of Derrida and a bit of Giddens, then somehow everything is there – it doesn't work like that, the ideas don't fit, and that's what's so wonderful, because there is a real creative tension in the spaces in between. This doesn't mean that all points of view are equally valid, of course. It's still important to make political, intellectual, ethical choices. The reasons for working with one set of theories rather than another are not just matters of internal logic, it's not just a matter of things fitting together: there are political and ethical choices you have to make as well, so that there are some theories that for me anyway must be not only criticised but *resisted*. The last thing I'd say is about the importance of meetings like this, of realising that other people have different sets of ideas that they work with, they have different agendas. If geography is to continue to be an intellectually vital discipline, it won't do it by having a single agenda. Perhaps that made sense ten or twenty years ago, but it doesn't any more, and you've got to have not just multidimensional descriptions – as I said earlier – but multidimensional disciplines which aren't dominated by a single set of ideas, a single monolithic research agenda. But for that to work I think there has to be maximum discussion, and maximum respect for the ideas of other people, and that's often particularly difficult.

Much of recent Anglo-American work in human geography deals very artfully with a huge variety of different theoretical approaches. But how do you make your selection – why Hegel and Habermas, Foucault and Derrida, for example?

Derek Gregory: There are a number of different ways of answering that. One is that I'm a historical creature, by which I mean that the people who have taught me have influenced me very much, I was made a disciplinary subject in part by the people who taught me, and who taught me geography in a particular way and opened up a particular horizon of meaning. But it's not just an historical thing, it's also a geographical process because I'm aware of all those other places I've been and the people that I've met, spoken with and talked about.

I would say that most of my research has happened by accident rather than design: I've never had a grand design (or not one that lasted for more than a week). And that has had two consequences. One is that I have learnt to trust myself and to try to understand how it is I work. I don't worry about setting off without a road-map to guide me. I don't worry, either, on those days when I try to write and nothing happens; I've come to accept that I think *through* the process of writing – I'm never just 'writing up' something I've previously worked out in my head – and so I've come to read the signs: to know when I *can* write, and to wait until that moment comes. It's not a 9 to 5 job. So learning to know and trust yourself is important.

Secondly, it's necessary to cultivate a kind of openness. I don't have a grand theoretical scheme or some great agenda that I want to set in motion, and graduate students have been especially important in confounding those dreams! I've been lucky enough to have graduate students who have always done their research and not mine, who have always disagreed with me, and who have always become close friends of mine. All of that has meant that the conversations we've had have been remarkably open. I've been very fortunate in finding myself in an intellectual culture which gives me on the one hand the freedom to be a trespasser, to wander around, and on the other hand the support that helps me to do it. I do think that a sense of respect for others is extremely important in all this. I don't mean that you shouldn't disagree with people. But I think that some of the most recent debates in geography have been vicious, ugly and brutal; it ought to be possible to disagree in constructive ways that are not personally hurtful.

But if you don't constantly open yourself to the ideas of others then you won't be working in the space between different theories, and nothing new will ever happen. My best advice is to be open to accidents, whether they are people you meet, a book that falls off the shelf when you go to the library, and constantly to keep open your sense of what geography is. I was lucky because I was taught by people for whom the question 'is it geography?' was a profoundly non-geographical question [...].

Could you give us your definition of the term 'imagination'? It seems to be an ambiguous concept – is it creativeness, fantasy or illusion? Perhaps concentrating on imagination and representation is a dangerously seductive approach?

Derek Gregory: You won't be surprised to know that I don't have a definition of or a single meaning of imagination. It certainly includes all the things that you mentioned. I'd want to insist on both the creative implication – that without an imagination, theoretical, intellectual, political, empirical, without that kind of imagination geography just becomes an endless repetition of the same – and also the psychoanalytic implication of desire, of fantasy, of the unconscious, so that I'm interested in the ways in which our representations exceed our intentions, and so to reflect carefully on those cultural constructions seems to me to be extremely important. Now in 'Geographical imaginations'[3], I began each chapter with two quotations, one from a novel or a play, and the other quotation from a geographical essay. I did this because I wanted to challenge what I think is a much too easy, a far too 'seductive' distinction between fact and fiction.

Let me give you an example. My PhD thesis was a study of industrialisation in England in the 19th century.[4] When I started the project I was going to use the concepts and the methodologies of systems theory. I wanted to study the emergence of the factory system and I thought that this would be a wonderful empirical example to explore that theoretical grid. But as I started to read the work of social historians, I discovered that there were really quite other ways of knowing the past, that the chapters that I had drafted for my thesis were really remarkably dull and lifeless. They were full of abstractions and they were full of diagrams with boxes and arrows and equations filling whole pages, and yet when I turned to the world of the social historians they were written like novels and here were real people, messing up this ordered landscape and making it irregular and complicated, noisy and crowded. So it seemed to me important to go into the archives and discover more about the people the historians were writing about. I spent three years doing that, and as I read through the archives, I started to recognise the same people occurring again and again, the same voices and the same arguments, to the point where I began to think that I knew them. And then I realised that this was a seductive fantasy. I remember giving a paper at a conference of humanistic geographers, people in full retreat from spatial science and systems theory. They all nodded their heads at the first part of my paper, because I seemed to have recovered real people, and their voices were speaking from the archives; but many of them were outraged by the second part, because I said, in effect, that everything I had told them was fiction. What I had done was go into the archives and convince myself that I knew these people, and I then turned them into – gave them voice as – characters in a play which I had written. I hadn't lied, I hadn't simply made things up, but what I could recover from the archives was so partial, so incomplete, that if they could have walked through the door and I were to say, "Ah it's Joe Smith, I know you, this is the kind of person you are", they'd have hit me in the teeth.

This is all a way of saying that the distinction between fact and fiction is something which worried me very early on, and that the reason that I talk about 'imagination' is partly to remove some of those distinctions. Behavioural geographers used to talk about the 'real' and the 'perceived' environments, for example: how they

---

[3] Derek Gregory, *Geographical imaginations* (Oxford, UK and Cambridge, MA: Blackwell, 1994).

[4] Derek Gregory, *Regional transformation and industrial revolution: a geography of the Yorkshire woollen industry* (London: Macmillan; Minneapolis: University of Minnesota Press, 1982).

ever thought they were going to get to the 'real' environment somehow outside of 'perception', beyond representation, I have no idea, except that the real was always supposed to be the scientific. Scientists were supposed to be free from perceptions, to be uniquely blessed with the opportunity to see the real; it was the rest of us who had perceptions, because that's the everyday world of fantasy and error and delusion. So I use the word imagination to get at the way in which we're *all* creative – scientists, people who work outside universities, everyone.

Theorising space[5]

Derek Gregory: For the past four or five years, I've been developing a course at UBC. Most departments of geography in the English-speaking world have similar courses, called 'The philosophy of geography', 'Geographical thought', 'Geographical thought and practice', 'The history and philosophy of geography'. Looking at the way in which that course is usually taught, I realised that it's typically a course in other languages and other disciplines. It's organised around a series of -isms and -ologies, so that separate weeks, separate seminars are devoted to positivism, realism, phenomenology, structuration theory, structuralism, poststructuralism, and in most cases discussion begins a very long way away from geography and then projects those philosophical and theoretical debates into geography. And there are a number of textbooks which are organised in exactly that way. Now, I've come to the conclusion that while that's one way of doing it, it's certainly not the only way and it's certainly not the best way. It's a mistake, I think, because it places philosophy on a pedestal and it assumes that different philosophies are like views from the tops of mountains. If you climb to the top of 'Mount Positivism' or 'Mount Realism', or sometimes 'Mount Giddens', you are supposed to have this wonderful clear view, and from the top of the mountain you can then shout instructions down to people in the valley below busy with supposedly more mundane empirical work. I think this approach misrepresents what philosophers would now tell you their project is about, and that it also misunderstands the nature of empirical work. So, for me anyway, it's important, yes, to read philosophy and to think about philosophical questions but not to do so in such a way that philosophers are assumed to have all the answers because they have asked all the right questions. It's much more important to engage them in a *dialogue* and even to disagree with them! There are questions that philosophy can't help us with, but that doesn't mean that we stop asking those questions. So what I have tried to do at UBC is to develop a course which is organised around what I call a series of site visits. It's like a journey, and at each site we stop and we look at places where geographers have done their most characteristic work. Now I don't mean that geographers are the only people working at these sites, in some cases they are joined by many others, but these sites are probably the places where we have done our most characteristic work: so we explore ideas like 'place', 'space', 'nature', 'landscape'; practices like 'mapping', 'fieldwork'; and we situate geography in relation to a series of other discourses that inform and enlarge our understanding of these questions.

---

[5] *Villa Bosch*, Wednesday, 25th June 1997, 9.30 to 13.00. As many of the participants were thirsty for 'authoritative knowledge', Derek Gregory provided a short introductory statement – emphasising the multiplicity of viewpoints, the need for crossing disciplinary boundaries and the necessity of making informed choices.

They are in a way conceptual construction sites, places where *work* is done – and remains to be done.

I see it as a journey across a very complicated map, an archipelago made up of islands of concepts which connect in all sorts of ways. The way in which you travel across the map, the 'souvenirs' that you pick up at each place as a kind of intellectual tourist, shapes the kind of geography you produce. And I talk about the concepts rather than the theories, because I find Foucault and Canguilhem very interesting when they suggest that some of the most revealing intellectual histories, some of the most revealing intellectual critiques, come from a 'history of concepts' – not the history of theories but a genealogy of these construction sites where work is done, elaborating and dismantling and rebuilding concepts.

So let me just say something about one of those site visits: 'space'. What I will do is just identify very quickly three phases in the development of our modern understandings of space and then spend most time on that third phase and ask you some questions about its implications. I begin by thinking about language, because many of the problems that we encounter in constructing concepts of space involve, in really quite fundamental ways, problems of language: most fundamentally, I suppose, the distinction between 'society' and 'space', but we encounter also the problem of translation itself. I'm quite sure that the English word 'space' doesn't carry within it exactly the same connotations as the German 'Raum', I'm equally sure that 'Raum' doesn't mean quite what the Swedish geographers mean when they talk about 'rum', and it's certainly not what French geographers mean when they talk about 'espace', so these are all complicated matters of language. But I want to make a distinction between two sorts of language system, a formal language system and an ordinary language system. In a formal language system – the clearest example of that is geometry – language operates in terms of purely formal qualities, it's ruled by logic, by a series of abstract operations. So, for example, if I were to give you a triangle with one side like this and another side like this and draw a line between them, and if I were to tell you that the square on this side is equal to the sum of the squares on this side and on this side, within a formal language system you wouldn't sit there and draw lots of different triangles, measure them, add them up and check that I was right; neither would you go out and build some triangles and see that that theorem is true, whether the triangles are made of wood or iron or steel or concrete: *it wouldn't matter* because all those operations can be conducted in the abstract. So, it's characteristic of a formal language system that the elements that make it up – the lines, the points, the X's and the Y's – have *unassigned* meanings, they are not tied to anything in particular. Now let me give you the geographical version of this. Imagine a topographical map with rivers, contour lines, railroads, towns. The first stage in constructing a formal language system is to remove all directions, all scales and all names on the map. Let's suppose we are interested in the spatial distribution of the towns. We remove everything else from the map except the locations of those towns. The first stage is then to think geometrically about the location of those towns: you might, for example, call upon various versions of location theory, central place theory, to make sense of their spatial distributions, but remember it doesn't matter whether those towns are in Germany, in Austria, in Wales or in the plains of Canada. The second stage in the construction of this highly abstract formal language system involves abstracting away from the fact that these are towns you are interested in; they just become dots on the map, so you can develop a series of what are technically called point-process models, a series of mathematical models [...], and at this level it no longer matters that those dots refer to places on a map, let alone places in (say) Germany, they're simply point locations in a geometric space. You are no longer even using location theory or central place theory, you are using various forms of purely statistical analysis to investigate the relationships between these point locations in an abstract statistical space. In English-speaking geography, for much of the 1960s and on into the 1970s, the belief was that the purest form of geographical science would be that which could construct the most abstract form of space, that could expose the most basic and universal of geometrical principles, so that we ought to understand space in purely formal terms [...].

The critique of that approach – of the vision of spatial science that you find in books like Haggett's 'Locational analysis', Bunge's 'Theoretical geography', most of the contributions to Haggett's and Chorley's 'Models in geography' [6] – basically argued that it *does* matter what those dots on the map refer to: it matters firstly that they are dots on a map, but the objects themselves matter, and you can't expect to produce a meaningful, helpful, revealing analysis unless you know whether the dots on the map refer to the distribution of towns, the distribution of measles, or the distribution of people with red hair. It *makes a difference*, so you can't reduce geography to a purely abstract form of geometry. This sort of critique was sustained by a renewed interest in 'the things themselves', and the things themselves were analysed for the most part using ordinary language systems, systems where the elements of the language have assigned meanings, so that *what* you are talking about matters. This involved geographers drawing on the vocabularies of the other social sciences, occasionally the humanities, but principally economics and sociology and to some measure anthropology.

And thinking like this, two things happened. The first was a division within human geography which repeated a division to be found across the whole field of the social sciences. On one side were those who thought that 'the things themselves' could be explained best using vocabularies of human agency, vocabularies which directed our

---

[6] Peter Haggett, *Locational analysis in human geography* (London: Edward Arnold, 1965), William Bunge, *Theoretical geography* (Lund: C.W.K. Gleerup, 1962), Richard J. Chorley and Peter Haggett (eds.) *Models in geography* (London: Methuen, 1967).

attention to people, either as individuals or as groups. And out of that emerged the tradition of humanistic geography, concerned with the world of intention, value, meaning, action. And on the other side were those who thought that 'the things themselves' could be understood best in terms of a vocabulary of a system, or structure, and out of that various versions of structural Marxism, of systems theory, were developed within geography. So that's the first consequence of these ordinary language systems. We find ourselves dividing human geography in much the same way as the other social sciences are divided.

The second consequence was that we became so interested in the things themselves, and in the vocabularies of those other social sciences, that 'space' was treated as a kind of result, a residual outcome, so that if you were a humanistic geographer you spent a great deal of time trying to understand people's intentions, people's perceptions, how people work, how people do things, and when you understood their view of the world, their representations of the places they occupied, their intentions in carrying out particular social practices, geography became a kind of cinema in which these understandings were projected onto space which was simply a screen and a particular place emerged as a result of their actions. The same thing happened in relation to various versions of structural geography, structural Marxism, structural functionalism, systems theory, where you constructed an elaborate social architecture. If you followed say Castells or Althusser, then you might have an economic level, which would be the base of the building, and then a series of political levels and then on top of that a series of cultural levels. Once the architecture was constructed, then a light could be shone through it so that the structure was projected onto the ground. What you had, again, was spatial structure seen as a result, an outcome, of social processes and social structures. Now, you might be surprised to find that I'm suspicious of those who think you can abandon a formal language system altogether; in fact, I think that some of the categories and concepts of spatial science ought to be reclaimed, reworked and made to tell very different stories in different settings. But I think the move to an ordinary language system was none the less extremely important: except that it had two damaging consequences. Firstly, the division between agency on the one side and structure on the other side, and secondly the idea that you could understand either agency or structure, let alone the two of them together, without incorporating productions of space from the very beginning: not as a residual outcome. I don't think that space is something which emerges at the end because that involves treating space as an object in itself, it seems to me that space rather ought to be thought of as a property of the objects from the very beginning.

In the 1980s it seemed to me that Giddens' structuration theory was important as a way of elucidating the claims that I have just made. I should say that I don't see the relationships between 'agency' and 'structure' as universal, as Giddens plainly does; I think that the relationships between them vary over time and often over space, so that I don't see one single model operating. But I do think it's important to try to find ways of incorporating agency and structure into our accounts, and this is a problem not just theoretically and conceptually, it's also an operational problem. It's not very difficult for me to stand up and draw diagrams on the board over there and tell you in principle how all this works, but the question is how do you make it work in a particular study, and that's not going to be resolved in purely theoretical terms. Giddens also accepts that you can't understand either agency or structure without understanding the way in which space is implicated in the practices that are spun between them. This moves us into a third phase – though not, I think, a 'third space'! – and Giddens was not the only person making these kind of suggestions: various people elaborated them in various ways. What happened through the 1980s and into the 90s in English-speaking geography was firstly a move away from formal language systems – space as pure geometry – and secondly, a move towards socialising human geography and spatialising social theory.

Now, I want to say a few things about where I think we are now, since we have gone a long way beyond structuration theory. My thumbnail sketch gives the impression of a single track of 'progress' and I don't think that's at all plausible (or desirable). Through the 1970s and into the 80s there probably *was* a sense that you could write the recent history of geography as one or maybe two paths being followed, with people shouting messages to one another through the forest, some on this path, some on that path, and that somewhere in the middle of the forest were the spatial scientists – eventually a GIS was parachuted down and they found a way out. But I think that most of us now accept that it's much harder to see those single tracks, it's much harder to identify a single direction.

I'm struck by how many of my colleagues who think they have left spatial science behind, still think in its categories, me included, how many of us continue, often in an implicit way, to draw upon its concepts, its vocabularies and its languages. Sometimes these languages are given new meaning by working in a different context. The obvious example is David Harvey; I think he's been a spatial scientist of sorts all his working life, but I also think that his developing work has been the single most important contribution to our discipline by any English-language geographer this century. And yet it's taken him in some ways not very far from spatial science at all: he still thinks there is a system of spatial order, that underneath the complexity and the apparent chaos of the world there is a systematicity, that there is if not a spatial pattern then a necessary spatial structure. His space-economy is ordered and organised [...]. More than this, he says that you really can't understand the capitalist economy without understanding the way in which space is implicated in its operation. But if you look at the concepts that he uses, and in particular his notion of time-space compression – which is really just political economy plus the friction of distance – if you were to read Harvey's work very carefully you would find, I think, that there are still a series of profoundly important geometric concepts at work. The other examples you might find more surprising. Doreen Massey's critique of Harvey entails the development of what she calls a 'progressive sense of place', in which we understand time-space compression not just as the world collapsing in at one point, but as something which is highly variable over space and in which different places are differently implicated in complex nets of economic, political, social and cultural relations. And what's the vocabulary she uses to talk about this conception? She calls it a 'power geometry', and again in the ways in which she has thought about industrial change and restructuring, the ways in which places are implicated in networks of various kinds, the language is a geometric, topological one. One might make similar claims about, say, Nigel Thrift, even Gillian Rose, whose attempts to chart what she calls 'paradoxical space' press into service the language of geometry, and on occasion even the language of physics. Now I make this point not as criticism, but to emphasise that the simple sequence that I presented to you at the beginning, encoded in a progressive narrative in which the past is always receding, left further and further behind, is really quite deceptive. Many of those early, 'formal language' concepts have been reactivated in the 1990s, and geometry now reconfigured as a social, political, cultural construction seems to me to be extremely important.

I also want to acknowledge that if you read the work of August Lösch you realise that you are dealing with a mind which could conceive of multiple geometries, not just one, and yet I think that the tragedy of it all is that the location theory developed in Britain and North America kept assuming that there was one single geometry to be discovered, there was a fundamental spatial order, which could be represented in the same geometrical terms. In the course of the 1990s we have come to appreciate that we live in a world of multiple geometries which are superimposed, which collide, and which can't be reduced to one simple universal scheme. When I talk about multiple geometries you would be right to be suspicious. What I mean by that is that for me some of the most interesting work at the moment is concerned by the ways in which space is implicated in the operation and outcome of social processes.

It's not easy to characterise this work, which is extraordinarily diverse, and reaches far beyond the confines of our own discipline. But I can highlight some general issues.

The first is a suspicion of what I call adjectival geographers, by which I mean a suspicion of separate 'economic' geographies, 'political' geographies, 'cultural' geographies, 'social' geographies. If you are interested in the global circulation of information and the part that the transnational public sphere plays in the project of colonialism, for example, is it an economic geography, is it a cultural geography, is it a political geography, is it a social geography? Of course it's *all* those things. And it may very well be that we have divided the world up too quickly into the economic, the cultural, the political, the social. So a suspicion of those kinds of adjectival geographers.

Secondly, a recognition of how partial and situated our knowledges are. In the case of Britain, which I know best, through the 1960s into the 1970s there was remarkably little interest in the world beyond the West, and the assumption was that the models that were being developed in the West could be applied to other places beyond the West with at best minor modifications. But as we've come to understand the history of geographical knowledges in more critical, less triumphalist terms, we've come to understand how extraordinarily arrogant that assumption was. We've also come to understand, in consequence, how partial and limited our own constructions of knowledge are. But I think in doing so we've also come to understand that there's nothing unusual in that. I've always been interested in the work of those anthropologists who have gone not to Africa, not to Latin America, not to the South Pacific, but into the laboratory, where they have looked at what scientists actually do. They have written ethnographies which show how science is carried on as a social practice [...]. Physical science, for example, is always located, it takes place in a laboratory, in a very particular site, with a very particular group of people, and a particular network is built around them: you can see this in studies of science as a 'gentleman's pursuit' in the 16th and 17th centuries and you can see it in studies of IBM in the 20th century. Successful scientific experiments depend upon site-specific inquiry; it's *this* lab, with *these* people, backed by *this* money, working with *this* equipment. Suppose their experiment fails. Now of course, if we believe some versions of the philosophy of science, when the experiment fails you just give up: the hypothesis is falsified. But of course real scientists rarely give up so readily. They tinker with the equipment, they alter it, they apply for more money, they bring in more students, they set them to work, they carry on, moving, adjusting, re-designing, re-running the experiment. Eventually they come up with a result, and it's published. Publication is itself interesting because you then have to produce a larger geography, in effect you have to show what you have done in this lab, with this equipment, would plausibly work elsewhere, and you have to publish it in such a way that people are convinced. What then happens is that other teams in other laboratories around the world, sometimes borrowing people from you, reading your ideas – so it's the circulation of information again – [...] try to reproduce your results. Seen like this, even 'hard science' proceeds on the basis of 'local knowledge' which, through the construction of these elaborate networks in space and time, gradually becomes more extensive [...]. In other words physical science is a situated knowledge too, and its success depends precisely on its ability to translate its findings and its practices and its concepts from one site to another to produce and fill these networks. It follows that the kind of universality that the physical scientists claim is an *achievement*, and it's a *conditional* achievement, dependent upon particular social practices. The same is true of any activity in the humanities and social sciences too. Whatever we do is always going to be grounded in a very particular situation, and we need these wider conversations to see just how far we can take it, just how far these ideas will travel before they fall apart.

A third issue is the increasing interest in attempting to develop an understanding of space which is at the same time an understanding of nature. And in case that's misunderstood, I don't think that means the integration of physical and human geography. I do think that many, perhaps most physical geographers seek to understand nature in such a way that concepts of space play an important part in their work, but I suspect that their concepts of space are radically different from our own. Conversely I think that there are now many human geographers whose interest in concepts of space increasingly takes them into theorising nature, but my suspicion is that we theorise nature in ways which many of our colleagues in physical geography simply wouldn't recognise [...].

The theoretical debates that you've just summed up for Anglo-American geography have – to some extent – had their reverberations here. However, empirical research and applied work have been much more prominent than sophisticated theoretical reflections.

Derek Gregory: We need to understand why this 'theoretical attitude' developed in Anglo-American geography. Many people who were involved in the so called 'quantitative revolution' of the 1960s insisted again and again that it was not primarily a quantitative revolution at all, but that it was a *theoretical* revolution. There were two main reasons for this. One is very much bound up with the sort of intellectual arguments that I sketched earlier, with some of the internal problems of traditional regional geography, and these turned on intrinsically theoretical, conceptual, scientific issues: on the explanatory power released by 'theory'.

But I think that there was – and still is – another side to this which is institutional rather than intellectual. I have in mind not simply the academy and the restructuring of what Bill Readings calls 'the university in ruins' as a special sort of transnational corporation increasingly and intimately involved in the commodification of knowledge. I'm also thinking about the ways in which what happens in universities is increasingly and intimately linked to what happens in the cultural and publishing industries. This is important because the 'theoretical attitude' of the new geography in the 1960s and 70s, and the fixation upon a rather different kind of 'theory' across the whole field of humanities and social sciences in the 80s and 90s, was brought about, in part, because 'theory travels': and if it travels, then it sells. Suppose I had spent my life within the academy working on Egypt in the 19th century. I suspect that if I had confined myself to a nominally empirical account – however scholarly, however complex – I would now have great difficulty finding a publisher because these are such strictly commercial enterprises and they would wonder: how big *is* the market for a close empirical study of 19th century Egypt? But a book that uses 'Egypt' to deploy supposedly larger theoretical arguments might travel much further. Of course, editors and publishers think theory travels because they think theory is rootless. Actually theory is remarkably rooted. Habermas may think he is describing 'modernity' but we all know that he is describing post-war Germany. Equally, Talcott Parsons claimed to be theorising 'modern society' but we know that this sketch turned out to be the post-war United States. Theories are much more closely tied to their contexts than we normally credit, but there is a claim to generality within this theoretical attitude, which means that ideas must travel.

If in the English-speaking world fewer and fewer scholars in our own discipline have devoted themselves to the study of particular places, the irony is that it's over exactly that same period that outside the academy publishers throughout Britain and North America have been busily publishing more and more travel writing: writing about particular places that *does* travel. If you went into a book store in Britain or in North America ten years ago, there would be a section labelled 'travel', but it would probably have contained maps and guidebooks. You go now, and the section on travel is four, five, six times the size that it was. It still contains guidebooks, but ones which now invest much of their space in the aestheticisation of place, guidebooks which are truly works of art, full of colour and illustration, many of them written by academics. But you will also find accounts of people who have been to places and have interesting personal, even idiosyncratic things to say about them. So there is this strange double movement. Through the 70s and the 80s geography in the English-speaking world lost its attachment to places and the people that lived in them. We found it increasingly difficult to describe what those places were like, and we assumed that if we were going to find a larger audience, if our ideas were going to travel, if we were going to speak to large questions, we had to do so using a stylised theoretical vocabulary; in this sense perhaps theory is the most imperial instrument of all, since the impetus to globalise and universalise within most forms of theory is so powerful. And yet in the same period the literature on travel – on the variousness and difference of the world – exploded and found audiences far beyond the dreams of any of us. As I said earlier: we really do need to attend to representation!

There must be some criteria for making choices between different theories, some strategies for conducting a discourse between the extreme positions of either absolutism or relativism?

Derek Gregory: I don't think that we should place philosophy on a pedestal, and we should not therefore constantly turn to philosophy as an arbitrator or a legislator to settle all appeals that are made to it as some kind of tribunal. It's not the supreme court of the academy, still less I think is it the supreme court of late 20th century society. Now that isn't to say that I think philosophy is unimportant or unilluminating, or that we cannot learn a great deal from conversations with philosophers. But I don't need philosophy to convince me that poverty is wrong, that exploitation is wrong, that abuse and violence are wrong – and if the philosophers are incapable of telling me that poverty is wrong, exploitation is wrong, abuse and violence are wrong, then so much the worse for philosophy! When I look at some of the philosophical disputes over absolutism and relativism, about whether it's possible to come to any universal conclusion or whether we each retreat back into our own systems of belief and leave everybody else to theirs, when I look at those discussions in a world in which millions of people are starving and are imprisoned without good reason, I feel a great sense of rage. So if philosophy can't settle those questions I'm quite happy for philosophers to go into another room, close the door and argue; but we can hardly suspend our decisions until they have reached a conclusion. We have to find our own way in the world without them.

Just because there are so many different ideas and approaches does not mean that they all have to be treated as equally valid. The first time you encounter a different view you treat it with respect, in much the same way that the first time you encounter any person you treat them with respect; but the more you get to know people, the more you realise that there are some who are worthy of your respect and others who are not, and eventually you make choices out of that *practical* encounter. By extension, very often we can't choose between competing points of view on the basis of some abstract philosophical principle, still less on the basis of Philosophy with a capital 'P' [...].

But to get back to your question of how one makes these choices, I would say these things: firstly, I do think as academics and as intellectuals we need to spend some time thinking about just what it is in our power to do. We need to understand how the academy is structured and shaped, we need to understand, of course, how power operates within it, but we need to understand the positions that academics have filled both historically and in the present, and that means that it's important not to have exaggerated ideas of our own importance. It means that there are limits to the academy and its political effectiveness. It means that we don't occupy some position of overview in which we alone are the people who can map out the course of a better and more just and more humane society. On the other hand, that doesn't mean that we shouldn't continue to say things about those questions. We shouldn't undervalue what we can do either, and I don't just mean that education is an absolutely vital and continuous moment in the construction of a better and more just society. Of course, one hopes that's true [...]. But changing the world is too important to be left to academics – which is why for the most part it isn't left to academics – but it's also too important *not* to involve them. So we have a part to play in that process. But the very least we can do, as we make our choices, is ensure that these ideas make a difference not to 'the world' but to our *being* in the world. There would be something very wrong about the project of a critical human geography that was full of exaltation, full of slogans, in which we keep insisting that the world is such an awful place, and that we must radically change it, and which did not require us to change the way in which we live our day-to-day lives. So for me, reading around two sets of ideas – around feminist theory and feminist geography and around post-colonialism and postcolonial theory – materially effects how I behave in the classroom and how I behave on my way home and at home. To be sure, these ideas might help people to construct programmes to produce a better world, but at the very least, if reading these ideas and teaching other people about them has altered the way in which on a day-to-day basis I meet with First Nations students in my classroom, if it alters the terms on which I meet with women, gays, straights – if at the very least it can do that, then that's something. There are of course less immediate, less personal and more large-scale interventions – the contract work, the applied work, involvement with government agencies and corporations – but none of them count for very much unless they also transform the way in which we *are* in the world. If, at the very least, we can do something about that, then we've done something.

I also think that it's important to say that we *don't* live in the worst of all possible worlds. There are things about the project of modernity, and about the operations of capitalism, that horrify me. But there are also things in our world which are not dark and sinister, and which it's important to retain. So my last point is that there is hope – we haven't reached 'the end of history' and there is still much to struggle for [...]. Marx was right, people make history but they don't make history just as they please nor under conditions of their own choosing [...]. And I think that it's important that students understand that however they live their lives, they are in some way making their own future. I also want to say that we don't just make our own histories, we are making geographies too, and that we haven't, I think, constructed concepts of space or concepts of nature which are really adequate to the promise of modernity.

Nothing of what I've said is particularly based on philosophical sophistication, and it's certainly not a rule book. I can't tell you how to make the choices you have to make, anymore than I can tell you when you meet a group of people, that these are those that you really ought to like and these are those that you should really avoid, because it's a much more practical matter, it's a matter of practical engagement and interaction. Those choices have to be made with an understanding that they have practical consequences, and so one way of thinking about and choosing between theoretical positions is not just in terms of their logic or their elegance, but in terms of the practical consequences that they have. That is, after all, the test of a truly critical theory.

And what about the idea of postmodernity?

Derek Gregory: Hovering in the background of much of this discussion of globalisation and of time-space compression is this vexed notion of postmodernity, which I have been careful not to use, and I'm careful not to use it for two reasons. One is, I suppose, epistemological, the other is empirical. I'm reluctant to use it, firstly, because the idea that there are these sharp discontinuous breaks in human history seems to me fundamentally wrong, to involve a conception of history, of temporality, that is far too simple. One of the reasons that I continue to find Althusser's work so interesting is precisely because it involves a much more complicated conception of time and historicity. Anyway, the idea put forward by both advocates and critics of postmodernity of an abrupt discontinuity, is something which I find profoundly problematic.

The second reason is that I continue to be both amazed and amused at the lack of historical depth to so many discussions of our late 20th century. I'm struck by how often the general accounts which are offered of globalisation – for example – could be describing Europe in the 19th century, Europe in the 18th century, Europe in the 17th century. Now I'm not saying that nothing has changed, but many of the claims that are put forward about the radical novelty of postmodernity, about systems of flexible accumulation, about globalisation and uneven development require much more rigorous and creative understanding of the historical depth of the geographies that we have inherited [...].

Modernisation, modernity and the city[7]

Various views of the nature of modernity have been discussed today – is it a specific period in time, defined differently in separate discourses, an idea based on a supposed dichotomy between traditional and progressive, a relative concept, an (un-)finished project triggered off during Enlightenment?

Derek Gregory: It's really two sets of reflections I have, the first are fairly general and then the second are much more specific and relate to the movie. Firstly, I want to suggest that modernity has no essence, no single unchanging meaning. It seems to me really useful to go back to Habermas's essay on modernity as an unfinished project,[8] because Habermas certainly traces the word modern in a number of different European languages and in a number of different dates. But he also shows that it doesn't mean the same thing in different times, in different places. I don't think he makes enough of that, but it seems to me extremely important because if we look at a dictionary of 200 years ago, and look up words that we think we know and look at the definition in a German dictionary, an English dictionary, and compare the meanings that words had then with the meanings that ostensibly the same words have now, we would find considerable, remarkable, and sometimes surprising changes. So this is to say that words acquire meanings in context, that they are not abstract universal essences. This is the basis of ordinary language philosophy, and it prompts two cautionary remarks. One is that we need to be very suspicious of the idea that we will arrive at a single, universally agreed definition of modernity; like so many words that we deploy, it has no fixed single meaning [...]. The other is that when a word like 'modernity' is used in a particular context, it has a practical force, it does something, so you have to ask yourself, who is using this word 'modern' and in what context and to what purpose? There is an extremely interesting book by a French sociologist, Bruno Latour, called 'We have never been modern'.[9] Now this is a book which is designed in part to stop the discussion of postmodernity dead by saying that it makes no sense to talk about being postmodern, not because you can't go beyond the modern, but because we have never been modern. And he makes that claim because he says modernity is a story that the West tells itself about itself, it's a mythology, it's used in very particular contexts to very particular ends: to legitimise a particular constellation of power, knowledge and geography [...].

---

[7] *Villa Bosch*, Thursday, 26th June 1997, 14.30 to 18.00. A lively discussion developed after a viewing of the short silent movie 'Easy Street' (Charles Chaplin, USA 1917).

[8] Jürgen Habermas, 'Die Moderne – ein unvollendetes Projekt?' in his *Kleine politische Schriften (I-IV)* (Frankfurt am Main: Suhrkamp, 1981), pp. 444-464.

[9] Bruno Latour, *We have never been modern* (Cambridge, MA: Harvard University Press, 1993).

Habermas's argument is that the project of modernity – associated with very particular forms of reason – has its origin in something like a contemporary sense at the end of the eighteenth century, hence obviously the interest in Enlightenment and Kant [...]. So it has its origins in Europe and it is, in that particular sense, a thoroughly Eurocentric construction. But if we follow it through to the end of the 20th century, into debates in China, in Japan, in Singapore, in Korea, in Taiwan, it's surely obvious that 'Modernity' is not being brought over in ships and unloaded at the docks – in other words 'modernity' doesn't just vary in time, but it also varies over space. Modernity has a very complicated historical geography and the different threads that people try to identify as part of the modern are tied together in different ways in different places at different times.

Now let's go back to the movie for my second set of reflections. The first question that occurred to me is to ask about the part that cinema plays in the story the West tells itself about itself [...]. Something very particular starts to happen at the end of the 19th and the beginning of the 20th century to the ways in which people in Europe and North America saw their world, to what Martin Jay would call the dominant scopic regime, and it involves a number of elements. First is speed, because surely the cinema enabled people to capture motion and to represent speed in arrestingly new ways. People had tried to do it in words, they had tried to do it in painting, but remember that one of the first exhibitions of moving pictures in Paris was produced by a camera outside a factory as the gates opened and workers streamed out. Now you might say, well, what's modern about that is of course the factory, mass production and a large disciplined work force, but what was really novel about it was the reaction of the audience in the cinema. They ran to get out of the way, they were scared that the people rushing towards them on the screen were going to come out into the cinema and crush them, and that's what I mean about the shocking experience of representing modernity in film. But there is something else about it, an attempt to make visible not just a fast society but also a fractured society, and in very many ways 'Easy Street' does just that. There are a number of different settings in the movie – the house, a police station, a mission, the street – and what the camera does is take you inside those settings and also connect them, and in doing so it makes the city visible in particular ways. There are, I think, two aspects to this. Firstly, we need to understand the difficulty many ordinary people had at the end of the 19th, the beginning of the 20th century, to understand what was happening around them and to make sense of the world in which they lived, because increasingly their experience of the city seemed to be different from that of other people, there wasn't a basis for a common experience, particularly as cities grew larger and as their social geographies became ever more complicated. In Britain for example, there were a number of important urban investigations conducted at the end of the 19th century, and many of their reports used not just the language of science but also the language of the mission which was taken from Africa and brought back to London. Commentators in the press, in books, even from church pulpits were saying that we know far less about what happens in our cities than we know about what happens in Africa. Explorers, missionaries and travellers had gone to Africa and brought back stories, vivid and important reports of life (and death), and much of the public assumed that they somehow – vicariously – 'knew' Africa put on display in museums, in zoos, in exhibitions. But critics worried that much less was known – as a matter of public debate – about what was happening inside their own metropolitan cultures, and so they called for those opaque cities to be made visible. So I think that in the course of the late 19th century you have a very determined attempt to make the city transparent, and it's no accident that the early movies were for the most part about the city, that they took place in the city and they opened up parts of its life to a more or less public gaze. But the cities they looked at differed dramatically one from another. 'Easy Street' is a movie that takes place in Los Angeles – would it take the same form, would the story be the same, if we transferred it to New York, Chicago, Detroit, London, Paris, Berlin?

I've said that I don't think that modernity has a single essential meaning, that it's context-dependent, that the word is used in different societies by different groups of people in different ways and for very particular purposes. For Latour modernity is not only a story that the West tells itself about itself, it's a story which always denies that it's context-dependent: it's a story which always claims that the knowledge that it's producing is universal and applies everywhere. I've also said that if we look at the part that cinema has played in the construction of our sense of the modern, it's bound up with an attempt to make an increasingly opaque city visible, to bring it into view as a 'space of constructed visibility'. One of the terms that relays backwards and forwards between these two observations is the notion of 'everyday life'. In much of Europe and North America the notion that people's day-to-day lives are ordinary, mundane, that they have a routine, what in the English language is called the 'daily grind', gains a particular prominence in the course of the 19th century, and it's marked by a whole series of developments including the practice of reading newspapers. But as the 19th turns into the 20th century the realisation dawns that day-to-day life is not something which is held in common. So in 'Easy Street' it was obvious that the experience of everyday life in that district of Los Angeles was fractured by class: you saw the middle-class women coming in on charitable missions to look after the supposedly improvident members of the working class. You could see too that it was fractured by gender: all of the people with strength, all of the people who were able to walk the streets without fear, were men, and it was always women who were being pursued, trapped, pushed into rooms and locked away. What you didn't see, surprisingly, is that it was also fractured by race: that's a surprisingly white Los Angeles on the screen, even in 1917.

So I think there are three things that we could usefully talk about. Firstly, who is using this word 'modernity' and to what end, what are the relations of power implicated in its deployment?

Secondly, how is our world – and the worlds of other people – *made* visible? Many sociologists suggest that we are now in a situation where the more knowledge we have, the more uncertain our world becomes. There was once a time when it was widely believed that as knowledge increased, so our sense of certainty would increase, that we would have a much greater command over the world because more and more parts of daily life and the economy would be mapped into it. Yet it might just be that by the end of the 20th century we're finding the more we know, the more uncertain we are in making our world. And thinking of the unknowability, the unsurveyability, the difficulty of taking in the picture as a whole, the importance of vision and visual technologies, you can see that a movie was a really good way to begin our discussion.

Thirdly, we ought to think about this notion of the everyday, the ordinary, which had become such a commonplace notion by the early decades of the 20th century. For if it was common, then, to talk about everyday life as dull, boring, monotonous – the return of the same, day after day – it may be that at the end of the 20th century many people now know the everyday as remarkably *un*predictable, *in*secure: far from being dull it's something which fills many people with fear because they don't know what's going to happen next. All things seem to be possible in this increasingly erratic, risk-filled society, so maybe our notion of the everyday has to change from a kind of routine, humdrum, repetitive world that the word 'everyday' meant at the beginning of the 20th century. Maybe now, at the end of the century, this notion of the everyday is something which – like modernity – no longer seems so stable, so fixed.

Mapping space[10]

Derek Gregory: Most conventional histories of cartography give the impression that the further back in time you go, the less accurate maps become, and the closer you come to the present, the more accurate they become. 'Accuracy' there has a very particular meaning, it's connected to an equally particular concept of objectivity [...]. Modern maps, which are produced under the sign of objectivity, under the sign of Science, are very persuasive – they have considerable rhetorical power – and I just want to give two examples of how this affects contemporary political struggles.

The first comes from the west coast of Canada, where the province of British Columbia still has far, far fewer treaties with native peoples than any other province. These First Nations insist that their claims to the land – land which had been forcibly taken away from them – be settled in the courts and by the law. Now this dispute is a very complicated one, it's still in process, but it turns in some substantial part on the politics of cartography. Several witnesses have appeared for the government, armed with modern, supposedly objective maps: and if you look at them you see vast areas of empty space. The implication is that such empty spaces could not possibly belong to native people and therefore the land could not have been taken from them: dispossession is made to disappear, erased by the blank spaces – the white spaces – on the map. But other witnesses, some of them geographers, argued the opposite: in effect, saying that just because these maps were professionally compiled using modern surveying instruments, just because these maps had been produced out of numbers written down in notebooks, just because these maps had been printed with such precision – just because these maps were produced under the sign of Science – it *cannot* be assumed that they are therefore 'objective', providing a 'God's-eye view' of a transparent space. They were, after all, maps produced by a colonial power determined to bring this strange land and its people within a white horizon and meaning drawn by a European conception of space and a European conception of ownership. These geographers have worked with native peoples, and you immediately realise the problem, because at the time of colonial occupation these were oral cultures, with no written record, so that these reconstructions all depend upon an oral tradition which is typically discounted by those mapping (and legislating) under the sign of Science. This oral tradition involves stories which one generation tells to the next generation, but these are not *just* stories. They involve vitally important local knowledge about which streams salmon will use to come back up river, about where

---

[10] *Villa Bosch*, Friday, 27th June 1997, 14.30 to 18.00. Taking up one of Derek Gregory's regional research interests, a conventional map reading exercise led to discussions about the power and politics of maps and from there on to a second set of questions about the concept of the region in geography. Maps used were the sheets 'Cairo' from the international map of the world (World (Africa) 1:1,000,000. Series 1301, sheet NH-36, edition 8-TPC, 1960).

the best berries are to be found at different times of the year, about paths to the hunting grounds in different seasons. Recovering this oral tradition and mapping its cultural geographies has involved elaborate cross-checks between the stories that one native group tells, the stories another native group tells and the stories that can be recovered from the accounts of European travellers and explorers – recording how they met people from this tribe in this place gathering berries or fishing at the mouth of this river. What emerges at the end of the day is not a conventional map and certainly not the result of taking out surveying equipment and recording down numbers in notebooks and reducing everything to a geometry. It wasn't a static vision of the landscape at all, but a map drawn on the basis of how people who lived there *used* those spaces. The argument was that native peoples used these spaces in radically different ways than those envisaged by colonial surveyors and cartographers, and a conventional map simply fails to capture that rich, diverse and complex experience. The judge who heard the first case refused to accept these claims: he believed in the incontestable objectivity of the scientific maps, and discounted mappings based on oral tradition, on this much more complicated sense of the occupation of space, as just stories, just myths.

The second example comes from Lake Titicaca, and concerns an attempt by the state to open up the area around the lake for tourism. Now, in order for this to be done two things had to happen. Firstly, it was necessary to produce maps of the region that tourists could use to navigate their way around the shores of Lake Titicaca. In other words this region had to be turned into – or produced as – a space in which outsiders could find themselves. Secondly, it was necessary to ensure that the peasants who lived in the region could be turned into exhibits on display, because the tourists who came to Lake Titicaca expected to see its marvellous floating islands, the reed beds, and the ways in which the traditional peasant economy and culture operated. This in turn meant that the state had to regulate the activities and movements of the peasants by establishing a national park, together with a series of regulations governing land use. And so the state produced its 'scientific' maps with grids and place-names, showing the road system which tourists would use to get to the region, maps which were dominated by the large towns in which the tourists would live, and maps which were dominated by administrative boundaries and zones and by sites where tourists could stop and gaze at the people on display. Now the peasants who lived around the shores of Lake Titicaca and who made their living in this kind of way understandably objected to being treated like animals in a zoo, and so they produced a very different series of maps, and again the issue was fought out in the courts. Their maps were not constructed 'from the outside', using surveying instruments and measuring poles and notebooks, to produce a view from the top looking down. On the contrary, many of their maps looked as though they had been drawn on the back of an envelope. These maps were composite views, comprising different geometries: sometimes the view is from the top looking down, sometimes the view is from the ground looking this way, sometimes on the ground looking that way, so that the peasants' maps tried to show the uses that insiders made of this space, a space whose practices did not fit the administrative boundaries and regulations of the state. Their maps typically removed the roads linking the region to the rest of the country; they also removed the towns around the edges of the map. The focus of the maps was always the villages where the peasants lived, and each village was shown with a national flag flying above it, so the clear implication was that these places were not enemies of the state but very much *part of* the nation. Again you will not be surprised to hear that the state won its case in the courts and that the national park was established. Here too the argument turned very much on the power of cartography, and the implication was that maps which are not produced under the sign of a very particular Science are not 'objective'.

Now, with those stories of mine, if you go back to look at this map ['Cairo'], you begin to see, I hope, just what a complicated web of power, knowledge and geography is presented here. What I want to emphasise is the claim this map makes to objectivity and the ways in which it turns Egypt and Palestine into objects. This is a view from the outside, it's a world made up of objects in which 'objectivity' depends upon the 'objectness' of space. This is achieved by telling you that everything has been carefully measured, by giving you a grid, a scale, and by showing you that this map fits in to a whole series of other sheets: in other words there is nothing peculiar about this map. What that little diagram on the right shows you, marked 'adjoining sheets', is that this isn't a one-off, there is nothing strange about this map, because the same mapping principles have been used on all these other sheets, they fit into the same jigsaw puzzle, all drawn on the same basis, and so it's objective [...]. The diagram of adjoining sheets is in fact a very powerful way of persuading you that this map is scientific, because in effect it says that this is just how this cartographic technique would show anywhere else in the world, and because the process doesn't vary over space, it's universal, generalisable: objective. Notice, too, that the map includes a 'reliability diagram'. This map is so objective that it shows you which parts of it are more reliable than others! In the areas which appear – significantly – around the very margins of the map, and which therefore presumably don't matter very much, reliability is remarkably poor; and once you have been told that, there's a kind of honesty there, people are saying, look, around here we are not so sure, but up here we are absolutely sure: 'reliability good'. So these markers and diagrams function as ways of claiming objectivity.

It's telling you it in other ways too: not least because it's printed. You could trace this map exactly using a pen or a pencil on paper, and if you put that map on the wall, and you brought in people from the street and you said, ok, which is the more accurate, the more reliable, the more objective map? They would all tell you that it's the printed one. So simply making this available and reproducing it, is adding to that test of truth.

I'm not altogether sure who has produced this map, it's British Crown copyright, it's published by 'Her Britannic Majesties Stationary Office', it was originally compiled and drawn by the War Office in 1949, presumably after the Arab wars in Palestine in 1947 and 1948. And yet it's also reprinted from a United States Department of Defence publication, so it's difficult to know where the boundaries of responsibility lie. But of course, you know as well as I do, that in most states the history of mapping as a responsibility of the state has its origins in the military. In Britain maps produced by the national government agency are produced by the Ordnance Survey. 'Ordnance' was a military term and these maps started to be produced at the very beginning of the 19th century when there was a fear that Britain was going to be invaded by the French, and so it was essential to map the coastline and the main towns for strategic purposes. And on this map you've got the same series of military objectives here, in which the focus is on communications, roads, railways, airports, the Suez Canal. Notice, by the way, that the Suez Canal is most certainly the 'Suez Canal', in brackets it's allowed to be the 'Quanâ el Suweis'.

The use of language on this map, as I have just implied, is revealing. The main towns are all given their English name with the Arabic in brackets afterwards. There's Alexandria, there's Port Said, there's Cairo, there's Suez and there's Jerusalem: these are the main markers for a western gaze. Now, the language is interesting in another way too. The map includes an Arabic glossary which translates the Arabic words which appear on the map into English. But what it doesn't do is translate the English words which appear in the key back into Arabic. So this is very much a map to be used from the outside by native speakers of English. If you want to know what the Arabic word 'Bîr' means you find it means 'well' or 'rock cistern', but if on the other hand you want to know what 'contour' means in Arabic, you will look in vain because the map won't tell you [...]. The area to the south and west here [of the sheet 'Cairo'] is the land of Michael Ondaatje's 'The English patient',[11] and if you've read the novel – or seen the film – you will know about survey expeditions concerned to produce maps just like this, maps which showed height, which showed the watercourses and the wadis, but you will know too, that those men and women who went out into the desert to try to map this landscape had great trouble bringing it into the English or German languages. European languages are very good at providing words for height, for watercourses, for valleys, but they are not very good at providing words for deserts. Many of you will know that the Inuit people of the Arctic have many different words for what we call just 'snow', and the difference matters very much to them. The same is surely true of the desert, this landscape

---

[11] Michael Ondaatje, *The English patient* (Toronto: Vintage, 1992).

which is shown as empty, apart from lots of numbers and names and the occasional watercourse. People who live in the desert are able to read that landscape in a much more complicated way, they can bring this desert into language in a much more detailed way than a map like this. All it does, really, is register heights and occasionally areas of sand dunes, whereas the peoples of the desert would presumably see this space in radically different ways: it certainly wouldn't be in terms of this road network across the Nile Delta and up the valley of the Nile, and these empty areas marked just by numbers would be full of shifting – and no doubt untidy! – detail.

Such a view of maps as powerful representations challenges the idea of cartography as an objective science and obviously has implications for judging new developments, for instance the use of GIS.

Derek Gregory: For too many people reading a map is probably still taught as a purely technical exercise. What we don't spend enough time doing is explaining that maps are, in addition to technical representations also cultural representations. These visual displays are extraordinarily powerful – 'a picture is worth a thousand words' – and a map must be worth even more and yet we've seen just how selective, how artful composing an 'objective' map like this really is. I think, for example, of the Gulf War and the way in which a part of the world was reduced to a series of maps, night after night on CNN, and it became a video game in which a bomb was dropped here, missiles came in here, and because it was treated as an animated but purely graphical display it was very easy to forget that these were real places and real cities that were being destroyed and real people being killed.

I sometimes think that the history of GIS begins in about 1800, when the French army of occupation in Egypt sent a series of surveyors and artists and illustrators up the Nile Valley to record and map everything they saw. The result was published in a series of volumes called 'The description of Egypt'.[12] This consists of page after page after page of maps and plates, and it's posed a problem for scholars trying to grasp its systematicity: but in many ways its organising logic is the logic of GIS [...]. Firstly, the plates in the volumes of 'The description of Egypt' begin round about the first cataract, and they work their way progressively down the Nile heading north. Secondly, when you look at each site it begins with a topographical map, and part of the map is outlined, and it's as though you click on the icon, because when you turn over the page or look lower down the same page, that little area is enlarged, and then when you look at that little area – part of a temple say – it too will be highlighted, and again it's as though you click on the icon and you turn over the page and there is an image of what that temple looks like from that position looking across the landscape, then you turn over the page and the next image is a close-up and you're moving in

---

[12] Description de l'Egypte, *op. cit.*

closer and closer and closer. Now, this sort of sequence is repeated again and again and again all the way down the Nile Valley, and one has this extraordinary sense of a visual display and interrogation of this landscape on a whole series of different scales.

Looking back at the disciplinary history of regional geography, would you say that it's still a research field that geographers should pursue today and how should they set about it?

Derek Gregory: Firstly I would say that in the English-speaking world most geographers would have no problem in talking about 'regional' in terms of a scale, so they would be quite happy to talk about the international, the national, the regional, the sub-regional, but you notice there that it's being used as an adjective and it relates to a scale at which processes operate, a scale at which analysis is conducted. The idea of the region, however, as an *object* of inquiry rather than a scale at which analysis might be conducted, is obviously a very different one, and certainly the idea that regional geography represents the pinnacle, the summit of geographical inquiry, the magic centre where everything somehow comes together, is I think problematic. Many of the most interesting, consequential stories that we have to tell involve moving *between* scale levels and between different places and can't be told within the confines of one region. When I was doing my study of industrialisation in Britain at the end of the 18th and beginning of the 19th century, I didn't see this as an opportunity for a classic regional geography.[13] Certainly the regional structure of production systems was highly developed: particular industries were associated with particular regions, cotton in Lancashire, wool in Yorkshire, coal in South Wales, iron and steel in the Midlands. And yet in order to explain what was happening within an industry that was highly regionalised, I had to keep travelling a very long way beyond the region. The industry depended on raw wool which was not obtained locally, but had to be brought in through networks of agents, markets and carriers from other regions and even other countries. The rise of the woollen industry in Yorkshire depended on its competitive successes against rival regional production systems, and so I had to keep track of what was happening in the West Country, for example. Its most important export markets were across the Atlantic in North America, so I had to know a great deal about what was happening there. Attempts to stop the growth of the factory system and maintain the traditional domestic system involved a series of political struggles that took people from Yorkshire down to London and back again, and involved a series of extra-regional alliances. In order to understand the radical change which in very many ways was at the heart of the industrial revolution in Britain I had to be constantly moving beyond those places where woollen cloth was manufactured, following networks backwards and forwards, into other regions, right

---

[13] Gregory, Regional transformation, *op. cit.*

the way down to London and into the Houses of Parliament, and across the Atlantic. That's a story which could never be told by treating Yorkshire as an object [...].

A still common distinction, at least for teaching purposes, is that between analytical geography on the one hand, divided into specialised sub-fields such as population geography, economic geography, social geography, and synthetic i.e. regional geography on the other, where – and this goes back to Hettner's 'länderkundlichem Schema' – all these separate geographies are projected onto each other in a particular region. This traditional concept is not concerned so much with scale, but makes you think more in categories, and it might therefore not even be a very helpful teaching device.

Derek Gregory: It's all very well for me to say that in order to tell a particular story the regional scale of analysis is often extremely important especially in terms of people's experience, people's day-to-day interactions, a kind of space in which people feel at home, giving them a sense of belonging and identity, and then to say that in order to tell stories about these regional spaces you are constantly leaving the region and coming back again [...]. We've developed a series of very powerful methods which enable us to connect the regional scale to other scales, and to conceptualise and recover the processes at work and the characteristic range over which they operate. We've developed a whole series of concepts and methods which enable us to follow these networks and these threads from one place to another and back again, and in doing so we've made the idea of the region porous. You kind of go out and come back and the idea of the region as a fixed object starts to become difficult to maintain.

All of this is very well and good, and represents a considerable advance over classical regional geography. But we have not been very good at dealing with exactly the demand that regional geography originally fulfilled, which is that it's important to give students a sense of not just their place in the world, but a sense of *other* places. While regional geography was, I think, a problematic answer to that demand, it was an answer. The world was divided into regions like a jigsaw puzzle, and you might object that this doesn't have the intellectual depth of a regional analysis that followed these networks all over the place. Certainly it was an approach that reduced the region to a container into which all sorts of facts were poured, and ran the real risk of thinking of regions as real objects. But I think that at least students did come out of those traditional geography programmes knowing a lot about the world. It became very fashionable to make fun of this sort of geographical knowledge: geographers were the ones who knew the capital of Brazil, knew how many sheep were in Australia. And yet one of the tragedies is that I meet so many geographers now who are really *proud* of the fact that they don't know the capital of Brazil, they don't know how important sheep are to Australia. I think that the political and intellectual responsibility of the discipline has contracted and that we have to find another way of giving students a sense of the diversity of the world that they inhabit, which doesn't reduce itself to classical regional geography. We haven't done that, we've got out of that by talking about techniques and talking about theories, and we have made tremendous advances in both directions, but answering that basic demand of teaching our students about – and teaching them to *care* about – other places, other cultures, and other landscapes – well, I think we have gone backwards.

KLAUS TSCHIRA FOUNDATION

Klaus Tschira Foundation

The *Klaus Tschira Foundation* (KTF) was established in December 1995 by Dr. hon. Dipl.-Phys. Klaus Tschira as a non-profit, tax-exempt organisation and was registered as such in April 1996 in Heidelberg, Germany. Klaus Tschira, the president of the foundation and honorary senator of Heidelberg University, is one of the founders and a member of the supervisory board of SAP AG, the international leader in business software. KTF is a major shareholder in that corporation. The dividends from the SAP shares accrue exclusively to KTF, and are used to finance its scientific and cultural activities.

KTF is dedicated to the promotion of science, international understanding and cooperation, the arts, and the preservation of local culture. KTF has support programmes for promoting specific projects in these areas. During the next three years the focus of the foundation will be on the support of projects in information science and economics. As an active foundation, KTF uses at least 51% of its support funds for its own projects. Of particular note are projects in the area of computer science and related fields of research carried out by the *European Media Laboratory* (EML), which was established for this purpose and is located – as are both the *Cross-Cultural Leadership Forum* (CLF) and the *Society for Cross-Cultural Cooperation* (CCC) – at the foundation's *Villa Bosch*.

The villa is named after the scientist, engineer and businessman Carl Bosch (1874-1940). Bosch entered BASF in 1899 as a chemist and later became its CEO in 1919. In 1925 he was additionally appointed CEO of the then newly created IG Farbenindustrie AG and in 1935 became chairman of the supervisory board of this large chemical company. In 1937 Bosch was elected as president of the Kaiser-Wilhelm-Gesellschaft (later Max-Planck-Gesellschaft), the premier scientific society in Germany. In his works, Bosch combined chemical and technological knowledge at its best. Between 1908 and 1913, together with Paul Alwin Mittasch, he surmounted numerous problems in the industrial synthesis of ammonia, based on the process discovered earlier by Fritz Haber (Karlsruhe, Nobel Prize for chemistry in 1918). The Haber-Bosch-Process, as it is known, quickly became and still is the most important process for the production of ammonia. Bosch's research also influenced high-pressure synthesis of other substances. He was awarded the Nobel Prize for chemistry in 1931, together with Friedrich Bergius.

In 1922, BASF erected a spacious country mansion and ancillary buildings in Heidelberg-Schlierbach for its CEO Carl Bosch. The villa is situated in a small park on the hillside above the river Neckar and within walking distance from the famous Heidelberg Castle. As a fine example of the style and culture of the 1920s it is considered to be one of the most beautiful buildings in Heidelberg and placed under cultural heritage protection.

After the end of World War II the *Villa Bosch* served as domicile for high ranking military staff of the United States Army. After that, a local enterprise used the villa for several years as its headquarters. In 1967 the *Süddeutsche Rundfunk*, a broadcasting company, established its *Studio Heidelberg* here. Klaus Tschira bought the *Villa Bosch* as a future home for his planned foundations towards the end of 1994 and started to have the villa restored, renovated and modernised. Since mid 1997 the *Villa Bosch* presents itself in new splendour, combining the historic ambience of the 1920s with the latest of infrastructure and technology and ready for new challenges. The former garage situated 300 m west of the villa now houses the *Carl Bosch Museum Heidelberg*, dedicated to the memory of the Nobel laureate, his life and achievements.

Text: Klaus Tschira Foundation 1998

For further information contact:

Klaus Tschira Foundation
Villa Bosch
Schloss Wolfsbrunnenweg 33
69118 Heidelberg, Germany
Tel.: (49) 6221/533-101
Fax: (49) 6221/533-199

http://www.villa-bosch.de/

PHOTOGRAPHIC REPRESENTATIONS

Photographic representations: Hettner-Lecture 1997

Plate 1 Derek Gregory in the *Alte Aula*.

Plate 2 & 3 Norbert Greiner, Vice-Rector; Klaus Tschira, President KTF.

Plate 4 Audience in the *Alte Aula*.

Plate 5 Reception in the *Bel Etage, Rector's Office*.

Plate 6 Preparing the lecture-hall for teleteaching.

Plate 7 Derek Gregory on 'Power, knowledge and geography'.

Plate 8 Seminar discussions in the *Villa Bosch*.

Plate 9 Group work.

Plate 10 Seminar discussions: moderation and documentation.

Plate 11 Outdoor talk.

LIST OF PARTICIPANTS

List of participants

The following graduate students and young researchers participated in one or several of the four seminars with Derek Gregory:

BANTHIEN, Henning; Department of Geography, Heidelberg
BECK, Grit; Department of Geography, Humboldt-University, Berlin
BEICHELT, Timm; Department of Political Science, Heidelberg
BÖSCHEN, Dirk; Department of Geography, Heidelberg
BÜTTNER, Hannah; South Asia Institute, Heidelberg
FREYTAG, Tim; Department of Geography, Heidelberg
GAMERITH, Werner; Department of Geography, Heidelberg
GEISCHER, Dorothee; Department of Geography, Heidelberg
GLÜCKLER, Johannes; Department of Geography, Würzburg
GOECKE, Kati; Department of Geography, Heidelberg
GOLDSCHMIDT, Bernd; Department of Geography, Heidelberg
GRANER, Elvira; South Asia Institute, Heidelberg
GÜNTER, Mario; Department of Geography, Heidelberg
HAHN, Thomas; Institute for Chinese Studies, Heidelberg
HAUCK, Thorsten; Department of Geography, Heidelberg
HEITKÖTTER, Martina; South Asia Institute, Heidelberg
HOYLER, Michael; Department of Geography, Heidelberg
JAHNKE, Holger; Department of Geography, Heidelberg
JEKEL, Thomas; Department of Geography, Salzburg
JÖNS, Heike; Department of Geography, Heidelberg
KIEDAISCH, Verena; Department of Geography, Heidelberg
KRAMER, Caroline; Center for Survey Research and Methodology (ZUMA), Mannheim
LIPPUNER, Roland; Department of Geography, Jena
MAGER, Christoph; Department of Geography, Heidelberg
MAYER, Markus; South Asia Institute, Heidelberg
MERKLE, Rita; Department of Geography, Heidelberg
MESSOW, Eike; Department of Geography, Heidelberg
MIGGELBRINK, Judith; Institute of Regional Geography, Leipzig
NÜCKER, Lutz; Department of Geography, Heidelberg
OESTERER, Martin; Department of Geography, Heidelberg
PFISTER, Grischa; Department of Geography, Heidelberg
RACK, Eduard; Department of Didactics in Geography, Frankfurt/Main
REITER, Michael; Department of Geography, University of Technology, Munich
REITZ, Verena; Department of Geography, Heidelberg

REMPPIS, Burkhard; Department of Geography, Heidelberg
REUBER, Paul; Department of Geography, Heidelberg
RICHNEK, Markus; Department of Geography, Zurich
ROTHE, Oliver; Department of Geography, Heidelberg
SACHS, Klaus; Department of Geography, Heidelberg
SCHAFRANEK, Mathias; Department of Geography, Salzburg
SCHMIDT, Andrea; Department of Geography, Heidelberg
SCHRÖDER, Frank; Department of Geography, University of Technology, Munich
SCHWAN, Thomas; Department of Geography, Heidelberg
TIDONA, Anja; Department of Geography, Heidelberg
VÄTH, Anke; Department of Geography, Heidelberg
WEICK, Jochen; Department of Geography, Heidelberg
WOLKERSDORFER, Günter; Department of Geography, Hamburg
WOOD, Gerald; Department of Geography, Duisburg
ZIPF, Alexander; Department of Geography, Heidelberg

Plate 12 Some participants of the first Hettner-Lecture 1997

HETTNER-LECTURES

1 *Explorations in critical human geography* DEREK GREGORY 1997

Please order from: *Selbstverlag des Geographischen Instituts, Universität Heidelberg, Im Neuenheimer Feld 348, D-69120 Heidelberg, Germany*   *Fax +49 6221 544996*